The First West Indies Cricket Tour

To Dave
Happy Birthday!
Much love, Shalot!
July 5 2013

WEST INDIANS, 1886.
(CANADIAN AND UNITED STATES TOUR.)

"The Veteran"
(Local Umpire.) L. L. Kerr. G. Wyatt. Mr. C. Isaacs. W. Farquharson. (Local Umpire.) J. Lees.
(Scorer.)
T. S. Skeete. Leo. Isaacs. L. R. Fyfe (Captain). P. Isaacs. R. H. Stewart.
J. M. Burke. E. M. Skeete. A. W. Swain. E. N. Marshall.
(W. O. Collymore was absent.)

Staten Island Match, 13th and 14th September.

The

First West Indies
Cricket Tour

Canada and the United States in 1886

———•✦•———

Edited and with an introduction by

Hilary McD. Beckles

———•✦•———

With

The Tour of the West Indian Cricketers
August and September, 1886
"A Memory", by One of Them
by L. R. Fyfe

Canoe Press

Jamaica • Barbados • Trinidad and Tobago

Canoe Press
7A Gibraltar Hall Road   Mona
Kingston 7   Jamaica
www.uwipress.com

10 09 08 07 06   5 4 3 2 1

CATALOGUING IN PUBLICATION DATA

The first West Indies cricket tour: Canada and the United States in 1886 / edited
with an introduction by Hilary McD. Beckles.

p. cm.

With: The tour of the West Indian cricketers, August and September, 1886:
"a memory", by one of them / by L. R. Fyfe.

Includes bibliographical references.

ISBN-13: 978-976-8125-86-6
ISBN-10: 976-8125-86-1

1. Cricket – West Indies – History. 2. Test matches (Cricket) – Canada.
3. Test matches (Cricket) – United States. 4. Cricket players – West Indies.
I. Fyfe, L. R. Tour of the West Indian cricketers, August and September, 1886.
II. Beckles, Hilary McD., 1955–. III. Title.

GV928.W47F47 2006   796.358'09729

Cover illustration: West Indians versus Germantown Club at Nicetown, Pennsylvania,
1886 (engraving). *Harper's Weekly*, 25 September 1886.

Book and cover design by Robert Harris.
Set in Adobe Garamond 11/14.5 x 24

The publishers and author are grateful to the Canadian High Commission, Barbados, the Toronto
Public Library, the National Archives of Canada, the C.C. Morris Cricket Library and Collection,
Haverford College, Pennsylvania, and Janet Caroo for photographic research and assistance.
    Every attempt has been made to locate copyright holders for all material in this book. The publishers
would be glad to hear from anyone whose copyright has been unwittingly infringed.

Printed in Canada.

Contents

Foreword

It gives me great pleasure to offer words of appreciation and welcome for this publication.

I wish to commend Dr Hilary Beckles and the University of the West Indies Press for discovering and re-publishing this fascinating account of a long-overlooked but important connection between North America and the development of cricket in the West Indies. Professor Beckles has done a masterful job in setting this account of the 1886 Gentlemen's Tour of Canada and the United States in a compelling historical context. His description of the tour's social and historical significance adds immeasurably to our appreciation of the diary and enhances its appeal as a delightful travelogue and game-by-game account from so many years ago. I note with some gratification, from this first-person account, that the Canadians seemed to relish the role of welcoming the gentlemen visitors to test their mettle against the leading Canadian club sides of that era. It seems they also showed their guests all of the tourist attractions to be found in several of the major cities of nineteenth-century Canada!

As the Canadian cricket team prepares to compete in the forthcoming Cricket World Cup, I have no doubt that they will be welcomed with the same hospitality and enthusiasm and will, like their West Indian predecessors, take back life-long memories of the experience.

Canada, especially Atlantic Canada where I call home, has long treasured its links with the Caribbean. Just as in those early days, Canada and the West Indies enjoy the closest relations through ties of family, education, culture, tourism, business and, of course, sport.

The Government of Canada is proud to partner with Professor Beckles and the University of the West Indies Press, Canoe Press, in the publication of this diary and the associated commentary.

The eyes of cricket lovers the world over will soon be on the Caribbean region as it hosts the Cricket World Cup, March–April 2007. At this timely juncture, I recommend this book to all enthusiasts of the game, and I trust that it will stand as a valuable contribution to the enjoyment of the West Indies' own "cricket, lovely cricket".

The Honourable Peter G. MacKay, PC, MP
Minister of Foreign Affairs and Minister of the Atlantic
Canada Opportunities Agency
Government of Canada

Preface and Acknowledgements

In 2003 I was invited by the West Indies Cricket Board, under the chairmanship of Wes Hall, to prepare a text to mark and celebrate the seventy-fifth anniversary of the first West Indies Test Series. The 1928 tour to England was placed before the world as a moment of significant historical value.

The product of the research project appeared as a book entitled *A Nation Imagined: First West Indies Test Team – The 1928 Tour.* It was a deeply enriching experience unearthing the socio-political details surrounding that tour, and observing the expert cricket writer and researcher Vaneisa Baksh devising strategies to present as a "docutext" samples of reports on matches from the British press.

At that time I was already in possession of the "memory" of L. R. Fyfe, captain of the West Indies team that toured Canada and the United States of America in the summer of 1886. I was fascinated by the boldness of these early West Indian cricketers who decided to take on the experienced Canadians and mighty Americans. For me, they were pioneers of West Indian modernity, stepping out from the boundaries of decaying plantations to contest a world they knew to be more vibrant and competitive.

Equally, I was impressed by the eloquence and humanity of Fyfe's narrative account of the politically complex "international" encounter. Aware that cricket culture was more developed in Canada, and that clubs in the United States had adopted a professional approach, I did not appreciate the extent of these territorial differences. It did seem, however, a fascinating project to follow the publication of *A Nation Imagined.*

The West Indies will host the International Cricket Council's Cricket World Cup in early 2007; the final will be played in Barbados on 28 April. It will be a historic moment for West Indian cricket. It seemed, furthermore, a compelling context within which to present a text that celebrates the first grand historic moment.

I was encouraged throughout this exercise by many persons in the Canadian and American diplomatic corps who expressed excitement about the possibility of recovering from history the tour document of 1886. Mr Michael Welsh, the Canadian high commissioner, especially, noting that the West Indies first overseas match was played on Canadian soil, was as keen to mark the moment as any West Indian cricket supporter. With his encouragement, arrangements were made to complete the manuscript. I wish to thank him most sincerely, and his staff, for their empowerment. The cricket world now has access to a splendid tour document that lifts from the late-nineteenth-century details of a phenomenal experience that has been buried, and largely forgotten.

The librarians at the University of the West Indies, Cave Hill, have been magnificent. The head librarian, especially, Karen Lequay, a great cricket fan, backed the project at every turn. But it was Alan Moss, a former campus librarian, who brought the original text of the tour to my attention. He was a diligent collector, and as a result the newly established C. L. R. James Centre for Cricket Research at the campus is custodian to an important and growing collection of unpublished manuscripts on West Indies cricket. I thank them for their support.

Janet Caroo, an excellent technical advisor and guide, worked on successive drafts of the manuscript, and she made the experience more manageable and enjoyable than it otherwise would have been. I thank her for the sacrifices of time and energy she made to see it through.

While I confess that considerable excitement did surround the passage of this project, experience has taught that undue excitement is the mother of many errors. I would wish to accept responsibility of any such discoveries while hoping that the pages will give pleasure to readers, especially those who may wish to ponder and reflect on the lessons, as well as the ironies, of the inaugural West Indian cricket journey.

Introduction

It took the considerable sum of £1,000, local currency, to launch the first global West Indian missile — fourteen amateur cricketers sent into Canadian and American space during the summer of 1886. Their mission: to play thirteen matches against club teams with deeper pedigree, and therefore expected to be bolder and stronger. However conceived, it was the inaugural "international" journey of an emerging West Indian cricket culture whose potential was yet unrecognized by the small but growing community of sport journalists and pundits.

There was laughter at the pier. Players from Demerara (Guyana), Barbados and Jamaica boarded different boats to travel beyond the warm waters of a blue sea that had kept them safe but second class within the expanding international cricket fraternity, which for near a half century had been accustomed to long-distance encounters. For the post-slavery Caribbean it was the first giant step into Western modernity, an intensely competitive imperial world quickly learning how to turn its back upon small places that were once of greater value than continental spaces.

It was a well conceived and executed project that imagined a liberating future few could see but many had desired. Majority thinking among West Indians with capital and connections promoted a stubborn clinging to memories of a "golden age" long crippled though not cremated by emancipation laws. The travellers, many of them economic members of the inward-looking, decaying sugar world, chose to break with the past and swim against the tide.

The tour was conceived in language not yet in popular use by the fractured and fragmented West Indian communities that had mastered the art of competitive parochialism. The cricketers boldly proclaimed themselves "the West Indian team", a strange, radical construction that stretched the mind across the Caribbean Sea, arousing a common curiosity while dividing passions along the way.

Since the early nineteenth century when the sugar industry had ceased being "don of the economic domain", and blacks were legally freed from plantation tyranny, West Indian men of "whiteness" had forgotten how to be courageous beyond the boundary of their account books. The imperial world they once knew and mastered was now considered a place filled with threats, having changed its mind and abolished the chattel enslavement that had long underscored their political and social confidence.

The post-slavery estate state of mind bred and backed caution. The campaign to catapult men out of their crease therefore, found neither private nor public investors. The money market ignored their proposal, treating it as a document dreamt up by devils and deviants. No priests were present on the pier. The sport seafarers, after the sounds of laughter subsided, slipped away in silent ships many wished would never return.

Critics of the northern crusade considered it a rash, ill-timed stroke, played prematurely by the ambitious and the reckless. They imagined the possible effects it would have upon society and concluded that it would surely bring disgrace to the place. It was a mid-summer's "farce", they said, doomed before it climbed on deck, and destined to lower curtains on a vulnerable people already engaged in the annual ritual exercise of erecting shutters against the ill winds of hurricanes.

The West Indian cricketers were not sailing to England. That direction would have brought an abundance of pride and the sweetest of joys. But no invitation was extended and no one dared to ask. England was the family home, but it had become a place filled with pain as it grew comfortable with withdrawing financial gains from loyal sons whose livelihood long depended upon the planting of cane. "Mother" was cold and did not wish to play with abandoned boys. Timid and tentative, they picked up their ball and looked north for a little sport with their ethnic others. They were not seeking a new mother. It was only a matter of time, they thought, before they would win her recognition, if not her respect. Until such time, cousin cricket in Canada was the game at hand.

The sugar boys were invited to Canada and the United States to serve an apprenticeship in which they would learn the bitter lessons of the international game. A mentoring in Montreal was proposed by the Canadians, and the Americans, ready to recommend a welcome in the form of a whupping, urged them to step up to the plate. The London Bridge was closed but the corridor to Canada and the gates to the United States were flung wide open. It was the kind of generous gesture only their continental cousins could provide, forged as it was in the fiery furnace of a common heritage and the shared imperial shaming.

It was less an outfit of carefully selected professionals than a team tailored to reflect the crumbling economic environment of the time. The West Indian economy was bankrupt, and the cricket culture it spawned lacked supportive organizational structures comparable with teams they proposed to challenge. Each player was called upon to pull his pocket and find his funds. The whites could rise in response, but in any event no one was ready to play with or against blacks. There was an operational apartheid at the outset, which had nothing to do with the inner values of the game itself, but with its colonial origins and nurturing within the slave plantations and imperial garrisons.

The emancipation in 1838 of two million black people was not, in 1886, reflected in a level playing field that was consistent with the internal democratic logic and egalitarian philosophy of the sport. Such a circumstance would have contradicted the racial agenda of the social game plan. As was the case in Canada and the United States, the black community in the West Indies loved and played the game. They formed their own village teams, but were financially and socially reduced and confined to the most parochial level of "representation".

How could blacks, not yet politically enfranchised, be invited to play for the "nation", the "country" or the "colony"? The social design and political framework of the game required much cash but no colour. The journey of 1886, then, was as much about hemispheric ethnic and cultural solidarity as it was about raising the standard of the West Indian game.

The best men did not make the team. The pressure of business engagements had prevented at least four men good and true, and white, from making the trip. E. F. Wright, P. J. T. Henery, A. J. Goodridge and R. Garnett, all star players from Demerara, the Caribbean part of South America we now call Guyana, declined invitations, considerably weakening the side. In the end just three territories were represented. But the concept of a "West Indian Team" was proposed and agreed by all involved. In this way, then, the West Indies was fashioned and internationalized as a nation within the sporting world.

On the cricket field the idea of a "West Indian nation" took shape and seemed as real as the nationhood negotiated by the Canadians in 1867 and won on the battlefield by the Americans just short of a century earlier. Canadians had eased from under the clipped wings of a fluttering British empire and declared "Dominion" status. The popularity of cricket in its provinces was driven and nurtured in part by Anglophile refugees from the American Revolution seeking a safer place from which to sustain the culture of "the old country". Without a flag and anthem of their own, and prepared to use those received from London, the West Indians played with great heart for the good of their homes and the betterment of the game.

They gathered at Montreal to play the first game. There, they found a society, diverse in social composition, with a flourishing cricket culture. In the city evidence of the affinity with cricket was everywhere. Yet the nation was divided to the vein over the legitimacy of the game's claim to official national status. The debate seemed desperate, if not deep and disturbing. The press inflamed the passions. The West Indians were embarrassed by the sporting riches of their hosts, who seemed indifferent to casting a vote against the competing claims of lacrosse and baseball.

In the midst of the furore, the Canadian cricket fraternity welcomed its guests with confidence. On the inside the temperature of excitement was not comparable with that recorded when English and Australian teams had visited, but it was warm enough to suggest respect and affection. The West Indians played six games in Canada between 16 and 28 August. They won four and lost one; the other was declared a draw. The Canadian leg of the tour was an outstanding and unexpected success. It was their first "international" outing, and they had done magnificently. Canada, however, can justly claim pride of place for inflicting the first ever match defeat upon a "country" that was to produce a team a century later that has been described as the greatest of all times.

Moving on to the United States, the West Indians played seven matches between 21 August and 14 September. Two of these matches were won, four lost and one drawn. The West Indians, then, lost their second "international" tour by a margin of four games to two. The whupping promised by the Americans was delivered. Completely out-played by clubs from Boston through to New York and Philadelphia, the tourists crumbled and conceded. To a considerable extent, these clubs had enhanced their game with the assistance of resident English professionals, who were also instrumental in the phenomenal rise of the Australians.

The captain of the West Indies team, L. R. Fyfe of Jamaica, kept a record of the tour and the following year the Argosy Press of Guyana published a book entitled *The Tour of the West Indian Cricketers; August and September, 1886.* A photograph of the team, taken during the Staten Island match, 13–14 September, adorned the inside cover over the caption "West Indies, 1886: Canadian and United States Tour". Missing from the photograph is W. O. Collymore, the Barbados lower order batsman; included are the local scorer and empires.

It would be inaccurate to describe the text as a "tour book". Fyfe certainly did not consider it a memoir in the sense that such works became popular during the period, and after. It was at best a gathering of press reports, personal commentaries, descriptions of social events, celebrations of dinner menus and match scores, prefaced by a nineteen-page introduction by Fyfe, who generously credited teammate Guy Wyatt, captain of the Georgetown Cricket Club, with conceiving the tour idea. Not wishing to claim any right to literary contribution he describes his effort as "a memory" of the team's experience, written by "one of them".

The *Argosy*, a leading newspaper, had also established a good reputation as a printer and publisher of books. It invested in the production and distribution of the text primarily for its use as a promotional tool for West Indies cricket. Fyfe provides an elegant narrative, written with the skill of a political leader wishing to empower all and offend none. Self-effacing and modest, he identified many individuals in Canada and United States who were central to the team's rich experience. Critical and insightful comments on the standard of play encountered are offered, as well as celebratory reflections on the many social interactions with charming and generous hosts.

The document has effectively disappeared from public view for over a century. The cricket fraternity, in particular, has lost historical awareness of the tour, and the lessons of its legacy are not generally accounted for. Daily, in the West Indies, references are made to the growing interest of Canadians and

Americans in cricket with no connections to this ancestral event. Official dialogue does not depart from this stance, in effect because it is now hidden from common knowledge. Young and veteran West Indian cricketers alike marvel when told the story of their nineteenth-century international beginnings, and react with disbelief to knowledge of their first overseas match defeat at the hands of the Hamilton Cricket Club.

It is hoped that an interest in this document transcends the boundaries of the cricket community. It speaks to the social, political and economic history of West Indian realities at a critical moment when the region prepared for entry into the twentieth century. Also, it is wished that it will be of some value to citizens of Canada and the United States who ponder the social disappearance of their former "national" game. Cricket is once again finding its way back into the living consciousness of these two countries. The recuperation of historical memory and the recognition that the politics of culture is as volatile as it is transient will serve the purpose of discerning the many stages and phases in the history of the Canadian and American nation-building projects.

The original text is reproduced without other than very minor editorial changes. An extended essay is provided that details the circumstances and context of the tour, with a special focus on the state of cricket culture in the three jurisdictions, Canada and the United States especially. Its publication is designed to promote growing interest in the history of the game in the Americas as the West Indies prepares to host the Cricket World Cup in 2007.

Like most West Indians, I love this game in much the same way that millions of Canadians and Americans did in the mid-nineteenth century. This effort to retrieve Fyfe's memory from the passage of time is intended as a celebration of the fourteen brave West Indian souls who boldly took the leap into the global arena through the portal that was North American cricket. The Canadians and Americans invested more heavily in cricket culture then than they do today, but the tide of time washes to the shore inexorably all that exists within its vast sea of experience.

These West Indians, as the earliest ambassadors of a nation imagined, were wined and dined as equal partners within the context of a sporting enterprise that valued the importance of human dignity and mutual respect. A century later, the tide has turned. It is now the West Indian moment to extend a warm and welcoming apprenticeship to their Canadian and American cousins as they prepare to re-enter the global game with pride and honour.

It is fitting, then, to end with Captain Fyfe's eloquent invocation: "Let us hope, as the result of our visit, that the bonds of sympathy which always exist between cricketers, no matter whence they hail, may be tightened between ourselves and the cricketers of the great American continent."

CENTENNIAL OF WEST INDIES VERSUS CANADA/ UNITED STATES CRICKET, 1986

The year 1986 might have been a challenging one for humanity, but for the cricket community on the "New World" side of the great divide, the historic date was met by silence rather than celebration. Cricket was not among the cultural package Columbus brought across from Europe, but the English who soon followed his trail have been so accused.

Within a short time the game cemented its place within the spaces that the English shaped, as deadly serious an institution as church and court. Anglicanism, business and cricket became the ABC of empire, the building blocks of far-flung English communities forged by military conquest. Cricket was a part of the apparatus of colonial governance, its social rules and playing regulations being as much part of a master plan to tame the colonized as it was a game to empower the colonizer.

The year 1986 was a politely forgotten centennial. It had been a turbulent cricketing century since a gathering of West Indian sugar planters and merchants, constituted as the first West Indian cricket team in 1884, made an inaugural overseas tour two years later. First, they journeyed to their confederate cousins in Canada, and then to the revolutionary Americans they secretly admired. Where else could they have gone? Determined to survive as a social elite in economically corrosive times, they found in cricket an instrument that could be shaped to serve their future needs.

The cricket tour was occasioned by the need to seek out new commercial partners and build sustainable markets. Also important was a desire to celebrate class and ideological solidarity that typified the scattered Anglophile commercial elite. As sugar producers they were fast losing ground in English markets where old doors were closing on account of free trade legislation. The Sugar Duties Act, which came into effect in 1847, was the first of many fiscal forces designed to bring closure to their historical privileges.

In the five years that followed the legislation there was a 30 per cent drop in the volume of sugar exported from the West Indies to England, a fall accompanied by a corresponding trend in prices and profits. In 1854, the English Parliament, now considered the enemy, made further fiscal and legal provision to allow sugar from "foreign" sources, the produce of other empires, to enter the domestic market under the same terms as its own colonial sugar. Considered an act of betrayal by the "mother", this development enabled West Indians, finally, to see the score on the board. They knew that the old game was over.

During the American Civil War, Cuban and Brazilian sugar producers, having difficulty accessing the American market, were allowed to flood the British market with sugar produced more cheaply with the slave labour West Indian planters were now denied. To compete with their cane fields proved near impossible, but to contest as equals on the cricket field, and to win, became a prime expression of the stifled, self-denied nationalism caged within their bosom.

During the 1870s, West Indian sugar producers experienced a further 25 per cent drop in the sale of their sugar to the British market. Their troubles were not yet over. They found it difficult to secure credit or loans because banks and other indigenous financial institutions were closing. They struggled to pay wage bills and to meet their financial commitments. Both the West Indies Bank in Barbados and the Planters Bank in Jamaica closed. The value of estates fell sharply and those declared bankrupt were placed on the market for sale. The British government sent out a Royal Commission in 1882 to see what could be done to rescue the planters. In 1886, in a desperate act of self-help, the planters sent out a cricket team to Canada and the United States to see what it could do.

No great bang greeted the centennial. West Indians had every good reason to make carnival of the moment, to extract from memory the story of humble beginnings, and above all to speak strategically about their standing in the world game. But cricket is a game played in the mind as much as it plays on the mind, and in 1986 Caribbean consciousness was far too consumed by the glory of its global dominance in cricket to be distracted by historic reflection.

The world was in agreement in 1986 that the West Indies team was at the height of its powers. The 1980s witnessed the rise of a mighty team that swept all before it in a fashion unknown in the history of the game. The English were humbled, the Australians subdued, the Indians and Pakistanis put to the sword, and the New Zealanders made to feel completely out of their depth. The South Africans had been sent into the wilderness by the world's sporting community for their embrace of apartheid. They watched from a distance, and trembled in their boots.

The experts were of one mind. The West Indies teams of the 1980s were the most powerful and forbidding of all time. Clive Lloyd's lions, as they were called, were likened to the perfect organism, a team with no discernible flaws. The year 1986 was about the midpoint in its fifteen-year rule of world cricket. The West Indian world rejoiced. The team was invincible. Society looked to the future. History presented few pleasures. The wounds of colonial times were still fresh. The past was a distant country, from which the majority within society, and the team it produced, were in flight. The year 1886 seemed medieval, consigned to the discourse of marginalized historians in a society that considered it had little within its past to memorialize.

Maybe the centennial had failed to capture the public imagination because both Canada and the United States had long turned their backs upon the colonial world of cricket, and had given preference to indigenous sport in an effort to build a nation with materials that had sprung from the native soil. Unable, or unwilling, to cut the umbilical cord, West Indians dug in and buried cricket roots deeper within their souls. That they should celebrate the first foreign step on the shores of cold lakes seemed as remote a concept as snow falling on their cane fields. If the pain of cane resided in the culture of cricket, the chill of Canadian plains, it seemed, could but add another layer to a history best forgotten.

But it had been an extraordinary century since that first ball was bowled on the club ground in Montreal. West Indian cricket has since broken free of the colonial scaffold, and constituted a natal, nationalist space for itself. It outgrew the bankrupt hands of sugar farmers, surpassed the mendicant minds of merchants, and found itself on the side of the sons of field-hands who saw in it an escape to glory. The cricket field, not the cane field, became the site of a new West Indian self. In 1986 these forces were still sharp, and too close to the bone to spontaneously sponsor sober reflection.

Maybe the moment carried no magic for West Indians because other issues that seemed more critical to daily life took centre stage. The region watched in disbelief, for example, at the fall of political regimes that hitherto seemed to know no end. In these societies the fall of the mighty is viewed with scepticism, if not suspicion, on account of the greater belief that a game is being played by the smart on the unsuspecting.

The collapse of the Duvalier dictatorship in Haiti, after twenty-eight years of father and son carnage heaped upon a proud, noble and historic society, was signalled by a childlike Jean-Claude boarding a plane to France where, it was said, he would come face to face, not with his maker, but his millions. The region stood, watched and pondered; for a moment even the passion for cricket receded and paled.

So it was also with the implosion of Dr Eric Williams's rule in the twin-island republic of Trinidad and Tobago. Since his rise to power on the wings of the People's National Party in 1956, Williams, "the Doc", had been the darling of a nation that was urged to imagine itself the freest state in West. It took a courageous National Alliance for Reconstruction, as the opposition political party was called, to remove the primordial People's National Movement from office, even though the "Doc" had died, in office, six years earlier. "Baby Doc" Duvalier and Eric "the Doc" Williams represented Caribbean political dynasty in much the same way that cricket had achieved its own long-term rule.

The proof, it is said, is always in the eating. Most cannot recall the day "the Doc" died, but many speak with certainty about the week the People's National Movement fell; they also remember the flight of a fascist from the ruins of Port-au-Prince. Largely ignored, however, was news that the unrelenting West Indian team had established a record by amassing a total of 360 for 4 wickets in 50 overs against Sri Lanka in the World Cup. West Indians were more concerned in 1986 with political matters. To the extent that they were prepared to consider historical issues it would have been the utter delight associated with the first federal holiday in the United States given in honour of the late and great Martin Luther King Jr.

The Americans, furthermore, were united by the traumatic experience of mourning the deaths of their dearly beloved space heroes. The disintegration of the space shuttle *Challenger* seventy-three seconds after launch on 28 January, killing on board all six astronauts and teacher Christa McAuliffe, would have shifted reflection to the still starry future of the space programme rather than the cloudy past of cricket culture.

In any event, the big issue in American sport was the International Olympic Committee's announcement that baseball would become a medal game in 1992. The symbolism of this item, it will be shown later, is to be found in the manner in which baseball won the American heart during the late nineteenth century, pushing cricket to the margins of the mind of the masses, there to wither and die as popular culture.

At the end of the year a popular Canadian television programme, *Twenty-four Hours,* polled thousands of Canadians and found that 68 per cent had paid no attention to the federal election campaign in that country. A mere 31 per cent gave a positive response. A larger number followed the exploits of the national soccer team during the World Cup hosted in Mexico. There was national remorse when Canada placed runner-up to the United States, and went down 1 to 0 to France, and 2 to 0 to Hungary. Cricket, alas, was far from the centre of the national sporting mind.

In some quarters, however, there was expectation that state officials in Canada would have found their way to mark the moment in some meaningful way. In 1967, to mark the centennial of Canada as a nation the Marylebone Cricket Club sent a team to play a series of matches. It was the fourth time the club had sent a team to Canada. The relationship between cricket and the state was rekindled.

It was believed, then, that cricket was on its way when Donald "Thumper" Macdonald, a well-known cricketer, was appointed a minister of government and leader of the House of Commons. "Thumper" was a more than competent player, and when in 1977 he played in a match to celebrate the 150th anniversary of the Toronto Cricket Club, it was hoped that popular opinion would focus on other celebratory moments. It was not to be.

For 1986, the register of cricket clubs operating in the country lists some 247 in seven provinces playing in thirteen leagues. These provinces – Manitoba, Ontario, Quebec, Saskatchewan, British Columbia, Alberta and Nova Scotia – had been receiving federal funding to support the game for sixteen years, and were showing good results in terms of membership expansion, particularly under the able leadership of Professor John Cole, president of the national cricket body, the Canadian Cricket Association, which was incorporated in 1968.

The principal focus for the cricket fraternity, early in 1986, was Canada's preparations for the International Cricket Council's trophy competition in

England later that year. As a part of this preparation, the national team had visited Jamaica two years earlier. The following year, 1985, the historic Atlantic Triangular Tournament also directed attention to the national agenda of rebuilding interest in the game among the youth. Canada, the United States and Bermuda competed for the Sir William Tucker Trophy in Bermuda. Canada emerged victorious, taking back to Toronto the Tucker Trophy, a fitting tribute to its pedigree within the New World cricket culture.

There had also been considerable celebration in Canada when the national team reached the final eight in the English-hosted Cricket World Cup in 1979. This was no meagre achievement. Canada was re-emerging as a serious cricket nation and the presence of its team on the fields of England attested to this. Furthermore, that the national team comprised eight Canadian–West Indians should have provided an additional impetus to join in recognition of the first West Indian match played at Montreal.

The same could be said for the United States, which had appeared since 1979 in the International Cricket Council's trophy for associate members. In 1982 the United States hosted the Marylebone Cricket Club's "B" team. Matches were played on the east coast against New York, Washington and Philadelphia. On the west coast they played against combined teams from North and South California. But it was in Chicago that they found the finest quality players. From the early 1980s there, teams had played for the Vic Lewis Trophy, providing significant cultural and sporting stimulation for players who participated in the inter-zonal competition.

In addition, Canada and the United States played each other during the early 1980s and found a fertile context within which to experience their common cricket heritage. Much has been written about the epic battle between the two teams in 1983 when Canada defeated the United States in Los Angeles. Significance was attached also to the US tour to Barbados in 1984, two years before the centennial, and the team's defeat of the Police Cricket Club, a prominent institution on the island that boasted among its alumni the greatest all-round player of all time, Sir Garfield Sobers.

The centennial, though, slipped by without any memorable celebration. Neither Canadians nor Americans placed any significant value on the grand event, and West Indians hardly noticed that the milestone had marked the beginning of their journey to excellence.

An authoritative publication, *Barclay's World of Cricket,* makes no reference to the tour of the West Indians. The details of the first Australian team tour to Canada in 1878 are set out, including scores such as the century made by Charlie Bannerman against the Montreal Cricket Club. Bannerman was a great player. He scored 165, retired hurt, in the first Test Match against England at Melbourne in the previous year.

Reference is also made in *Barclay's World of Cricket* to the first Canadian side that toured England in 1880, and the follow-up tour of 1887. The Canadian public, impressed with the fact that its entire team was made up of locally born players, celebrated the victories of the team against Ireland, and three counties: Leicestershire, Warwickshire and Derbyshire. After describing these encounters the *Barclay's World of Cricket* moved on to the 1905 return tour of the Marylebone Cricket Club to Canada, overlooking the West Indians of 1886.

The same was true for the United States. The details of the English tour of 1859 and the impact of the Civil War on the popularity of the game are outlined with gripping clarity by writers in the Barclay's book. So too are the accounts of the 1868 tour of the English team. The documentation then moves suddenly to the Australian tour of 1896 and the American tour to England the following year, which was classified as first class. A full-page image of the great American swing bowler, J. Barton King, who toured England on three occasions between 1893 and 1908, signals the importance of these events to the editors.

It could be, also, that Canadian and American cricketers considered the West Indian tour of little consequence to their rapidly emerging international status. The West Indians had not yet made a tour to England, as clear an indication as any of their marginal ranking. The Americans were certainly more developed in terms of performance and facilities, and the Canadians were not far behind. Silence around the tour, then, probably signalled recognition that its significance is to be found more in its commercial aspect than as a serious encounter of cricketing "nations".

CANADIAN BACKGROUND TO THE WEST INDIAN TOUR

The West Indians arrived at Montreal to play their first overseas game on 16 August 1886. They found a highly developed cricket culture, in most respects more advanced than what they had left behind. The Canadians had been playing organized cricket for a longer period. They greeted the West Indians with an air of confidence derived from knowledge of this history.

Cricket was extensively played in all the provinces from the Atlantic to the Pacific. It was recognized by the state as a core part of the emerging national culture. Sir John A. MacDonald, the first prime minister of the confederate nation that came into being in 1867, was keen to provide national society with a sporting reference. With the full support of his cabinet, he took what seemed a logical step, and declared cricket the national game. It was as much recognition of the popularity of the game as it was a validation of Englishness as a foundation stone on which the young nation would be built.

Two other games, lacrosse and baseball, competed in 1867 for the status of national game, but the evidence indicated clearly that cricket was ahead on all counts. The debate carried in the press reflected views expressed in homes and in the streets. Lacrosse was undoubtedly popular in the Montreal area that welcomed the West Indians, and baseball was fast penetrating the expanding towns of southern Ontario, but cricket had no serious rival in the wider Ontario, most of Quebec and the Maritime Provinces.

Canadians had grown to take pride in the development of their local cricket teams, and the idea that a national team would one day hold its own against England stimulated their imagination. But there were detractors, keen to play the "colonial card", attaching to cricketers a mentality crippled by imperial mimicry. George Beers, for example, in a series of articles published by the *Montreal Gazette* in 1867, argued that "cricket, wherever played by Britons, is a link of loyalty to bind them to their home and so may Lacrosse be to Canadians". Furthermore, he said, "we may yet find it will do as much for our young Dominion as the Olympic Games did for Greece or cricket for our Motherland".[1]

The official endorsement of cricket at the outset of the nation-building project was a hard-won achievement by cricketers who had kept the game alive even in the most hostile physical environments. As was the case in the West Indies, it incubated within the military complex of army and navy, with officers promoting its wider culture as an asset in the development of masculinity. They played on ship decks and on frozen rivers and lakes. Jon Harris, in a succinct historical overview of the game's development, noted:

> During an exploration, under the command of Capt. William Parry, two Royal Navy vessels, seeking the Northwest Passage, became stuck in the ice. There is record of cricket (in the form of a print from an engraving), being played on ice in 1822–23 near the island of Igloolik at a latitude of 3 degrees north of the Arctic Circle. These games were certainly the venue of the first cricket played in Canada's far north, and because it is the land of the midnight sun, it is assumed that there was no delay in the game due to bad light.[2]

The Arctic escapades of naval crew notwithstanding, Canadian cricket grew to maturity in settled community environments, though many of them were sustained by the overwhelming presence of military personnel. Late-eighteenth-century Canada was a frontier that experienced the impact of transient characters as well as stationed troops. Even though there were military garrisons established in Halifax, Quebec City and Toronto in 1749, 1759 and 1792 respectively, in which cricket was played, it was the city of Montreal that claimed home to the first cricket match in which settlers rather than soldiers played. The site of this first civilian match was Ile Ste-Helene, on the outskirts of Montreal, in 1785, two decades before match records made an appearance in Caribbean archives.

But it was Toronto, the city built upon the military complex of Fort York, that forged ahead as the vibrant centre of Canadian cricket during the nineteenth century, a reputation it enjoys to this day. As in England and the Caribbean, the Canadian grammar schools provided an efficient vehicle on which cricket travelled into the modern era. The establishment of the Home District Grammar School in Toronto in 1807 proved a catalyst among the youth, a development that assured the game a special place within the social world of young males from the elite classes.

With the backing of the academic community, George A. Barder secured financial and civic support to establish the Toronto Cricket Club in 1827, an institution that did much to popularize the game. The St John community in New Brunswick continues to argue, however, that its cricket club, established in 1828, was first in Canada to organize competitive matches. What is not disputed is that Barder is considered the founding father of modern Canadian cricket, and most writers such as Jon Harris, Keith Sandiford and Deb K. Das have acknowledged his pioneering work as a cricket organizer and promoter.[3]

Within a decade of Barder's initiative, organized cricket had spread to other provinces. Clubs based on the Toronto model emerged in Hamilton, Woodstock and Guelph. These clubs were ably assisted by Barder's generous support and leadership. The most prestigious of these clubs was established in 1840 in the town of Ottawa, and took the name "Carleton Cricket Club". This was a significant development. It proved so successful an institution for the professional classes, spawned by the grammar schools and colleges, that within a short time the town was able to host visiting teams from the Prescott Cricket Club and the Aylmer Cricket Club.

The Canadian public schools, conceived as a part of an imagined English system, embraced cricket culture for much the same reason that English educators did. Concepts embedded within the game, such as "loyalty to the leader", "playing for the team", and "respect for rules and official decisions", were promoted as core values in nation-building, and best inculcated within the minds of the young. In this regard, cricket was celebrated as an effective sporting incubator of establishment cultural values.

During the decades before Dominion status, no education institution invested as heavily in the ideological world of cricket as Upper Canada College. The College Cricket Club was established in 1836, with an executive dominated by the political and professional elite. Its patron was the colourful character, Sir Francis Bond, who at the time held the influential office of lieutenant governor of Upper Canada. In addition, George Barder, a supporter of the idea of college cricket, saw to it that frequent matches were organized against the Toronto Cricket Club. Town and gown, then, combined to consolidate the official standing and community popularity of cricket.

According to Kenneth R. Bullock, a leading writer of Canadian cricket history, "the first match of which there is any record took place in Hamilton between Toronto and Guelph" in 1834. The following year, he tells us, there are full scores of a match between the same teams, played in Guelph on 15 August. In 1836 the records again reveal the guiding hand of Barder, this time as the organizer of a series between the Toronto Cricket Club and Upper Canada College.[4]

CRICKET CLUBS ESTABLISHED IN CANADA, 1870–1894

13th Hussars	Flamborough West	Prescott
16th Regiment	Florence	Rosedale
43rd Light Infantry	Galt	Sarnia
52nd Regiment	Garrison	Sawbones
82nd Regiment	Guelph	Simcoe
85th/ 43rd Officer	Hamilton	St Catharines
Amherstburg	Ingersoll	St Mary's
Arkona	Kingston	Stratford
Aurora	Leamington	Strathroy
Bankers of Ontario	Lincoln/Wellington	Toronto
Barrie	Lindsay	Toronto Garrison
Belleville	Listowel	Toronto Junction
Berlin	London	Trinity College
Blytheswood	London Asylum	Trinity College School
Bracebridge	Middlesex County	University of Toronto
Brantford	Mooretown	Upper Canada College
Brockville	Napanee	Uxbridge
Colborne	Niagara	W.A. Murray & Co.
Carleton	Oakville	Wallaceburg
Chatham	Oil Springs	Watford
Cobourg	Orillia	Welland
Collingwood	Ottawa	Whitby
Darlington	Parkdale	Windsor
Dawn Mills	Paris	Woodstock
Dundas	Peterborough	Wyoming
East Toronto	Port Hope	Yonge St.

Nowhere in the West Indies had cricket reached this level of organization. In every respect the Canadians had taken the lead. What seems to be the earliest record of a cricket game in the West Indies, and certainly for Barbados, according to Warren Alleyne, is found in the *Barbados Mercury and Bridgetown Gazette* of Saturday 17 January 1808. This consists of a notice in the newspaper inserted by J. C. Coleman, inviting members to dine the following Tuesday at two o'clock in the afternoon.[5]

In 1809, the public was also invited to attend a "grand cricket match to be played between the officers of the Royal West Indies Rangers and the third West India Regiment for 65 guineas a side, on the Grand Parade (St Ann's Garrison Savannah) on Tuesday 19th". One team was required to wear "flannel and blue facings" and the other "flannel and yellow Facing".

It took much longer in the West Indies for cricket to spill from the garrisons into civil society. When it did the cane fields of plantations and the urban villages were waiting to become the organizing units. This process was four decades in the making. In 1849 the gentlemen of the parish of St Michael, in which St Ann's is located, constituted themselves into two "cricket companies", the "City" club and the "St Michael" club. The editor of the *Barbadian,* a leading newspaper, described the first game between these two clubs as an affair watched by "highly respectable ladies and gentlemen" that "evinced great spirit and extreme goodwill".

Unlike the Canadian clubs, however, the early West Indian clubs were not equipped with facilities such as pavilions for official patrons, members and players. Arrangements were crude and ad hoc. The game played between the two Barbados clubs took place on a specially prepared pitch at Constant plantation, owned by Mr Prettijohn. As host of the game, Prettijohn cleared an opening in a cane field, erected tents for special guests and provided refreshment in an open space for spectators. It was known in the West Indies that such temporary arrangements fell well short of what was already the standard in Canada and the United States.

By 1849 the Canadians were already engaged in international tours. In 1844 Canada and the United States met in their first international. "This was over 30 years before the famed England v Australia series began", writes Bullock, "and historians believe the contest is the oldest international sporting fixture in the world". The first English team visited Canada in 1859, and between that time and the end of the century, seventeen touring teams visited the country, establishing its reputation as an important and lucrative venue for the international game.[6]

Of these seventeen cricket teams that toured, eleven were from England, two from Australia, three from Ireland and one from the West Indies. The performance record of Canada in these tours suggests at best a modest showing. Refusing to promote a professional culture within the game, and clinging to the concept of the amateur player, Canada was easily dominated by England, which sent out players from its growing professional community. Canada won but one of the forty-two games in these series for which we have records, losing thirty-one and drawing ten. What was respected about Canada's involvement, however, was it unshakable commitment to the advancement of the game and the pursuit of excellence.

Neither lacrosse nor baseball was able to attract such international attention and sporting respect. The promotional material for the 1844 club encounter highlighted the international dimensions of the engagement, and made reference to Canada versus United States as the organizing concept. The composition of teams, however, suggests that it was more a contest between the Toronto Cricket Club and the St George's Club in New York. The match was played, says the *Toronto Herald,* at the St George's Club's ground in Bloomingdale Park before a crowd of about five thousand. The American media, on the other hand, reported a crowd of twenty thousand. Prize money, says the *Herald,* was $100,000; the American media make reference to $120,000.

The West Indians, meanwhile, were a considerable distance behind with respect to the establishment of basic infrastructure. The struggle to secure financial support for the game frustrated players and spectators alike. Spectators especially were growing cynical about the ability of official patrons to rise to Canadian and American standards, already known throughout the region. The patronage of colonial governors and the occasional appearances of members of the royal family proved insufficient.

Raising funds for cricket clubs seemed less important than pooling financial resources to establish the mutual assurance societies that sprung up almost everywhere in the region in the aftermath of emancipation. The focus of these financial institutions was to secure indigenous investment funds to keep the locally owned sugar estates out of bankruptcy, and ultimately from the clutching hands of English merchants with a rising appetite for West Indian plantation properties. Canadian and American cricketers were spared such concerns for at least another decade. Anti-slavery forces had not yet taken control of the national sensibility. Cricket continued to flourish within the white communities while enslaved blacks laboured in the mines, fields and forests.

There were no cricket clubs with developed facilities and dedicated management in the West Indies in 1859, when the Canadians hosted a team of touring English professionals. Jamaica proudly proclaimed two clubs, both formed in 1857, the St Jago Club, and the Vere and Clarendon Club. None, however, had a profile beyond their community and neither participated in organized competition. By the time the Kingston Club was established in 1863, however, Jamaican cricket was well on its way, with leagues emerging and facilities developing.

The 1859 tour of an English team was considered Canada's moment of arrival on the international stage. The English were respectful of the quality of Canadian players, and they sent out a strong team made up of noted players with already high reputations. The team was led by the well-known George Parr of Nottinghamshire, who was a favourite with the ladies on account of his graceful style and charming wit. Matches were played in Montreal and Hamilton. Canada represented itself well enough, though the tourists won the day. The English moved on to the United States, where they played matches in Rochester, New York, defeating in the process a combined Canada–United States team. Canada, then, can rightly claim the honour of being the first nation to host a visiting professional international cricket team.

The impact of the 1859 tour was considerable. Reports of growing numbers of school boys and young men playing in the parks suggest that the game had taken hold of the society in a way that no other sport had done. In sections of the press, however, it was reported that the heavy defeats at the hands of the English damaged the reputation of Canadian cricket, and that tour organizers were wrong to overstep the crease in pitting amateurs against professionals. More persuasive were replies that showed how the tour served the necessary purpose of exposing Canadian players to the highest international standard. Bullock has argued that the impact of the tour was to promote the spread of the game beyond the confines of Toronto. He states:

> During these years of healthy cricket activities in the east, the game was spreading rapidly in the west. In 1864 the North West Cricket Club was formed at Winnipeg and in 1876 the famous Victoria Cricket Club was formed on the west coast. Cricket had already been played in both areas prior to the formation of these two clubs, but the game was now beginning to take hold in the west and as a result the sport was being played from coast to coast.[7]

The West Indians, meanwhile, began intra-regional competition in 1865. The colonies of Jamaica, Barbados, Trinidad and Guyana competed with each other for regional supremacy. Two years later Canada achieved dominion status and proclaimed its right to a national team. The Canadians, then, were playing nation-cricket while the West Indians played the colonial version. While the Canadian state had declared cricket the national game, and invested resources in its development, West Indian elites were debating whether blacks and coloureds should be integrated into the sport as equal on-field participants.

Empowered with the confidence derived from official validation, Canadian cricket managers moved into the global leadership of the game. They prepared to make their boldest move yet, one that would win widespread support within the young nation and repay the prime minister for his noble gesture of declaring cricket the national sport. In 1872 cricket officials welcomed the third English team to the country. There was considerable pomp and ceremony. Canadians travelled the length of the country to welcome the English team and witness its engagement with their emerging national side.

But there was more, much more. Among the English tourists to Canada was the great W. G. Grace, easily the world's most renowned and respected cricketer. "WG" was a legend wherever the game was played. To see him on the field was to witness the spectacle of a lifetime. The event signalled that Canadian cricket had arrived at a very early stage in the vanguard of the global game. It was a proud moment, one that showered considerable prestige upon the nation.

Grace's visit was an enormous success. He complimented the players of the Toronto side as he bashed their bowlers around the park in a swashbuckling innings of 142. The English gave local teams a sound beating. In celebration of the contribution to cricket of the University of Toronto, the last game was played at the campus. It was a festive occasion, with teams mixed from English and Canadian players. This was an example of the touch of "class" the public had come to expect of cricketers.

Grace left an impression upon the cricketing community. Stories of the tour became the stuff of legend. Thousands who did not see Grace's innings described it in great detail in bars, homes and restaurants. Millions claimed to have met the great man. Cricket in Canada had acquired its own pantheon of myths and feisty folklore.

Next in line to tour Canada were the Australians. This was a logical development, given that England, and to a lesser extent Australia, were considered the superpowers of the game. W. L. Murdoch's Australian team arrived in 1878. It was on its way home after a long, well-patronized tour of the English counties. The Aussies had good reason to feel themselves second only to England, but not by much. They had defeated nine of the strongest county teams and had struck a telling blow when they put the Marylebone Cricket Club to the sword at Lord's.

Like the English team, the Aussies travelled with stars whose reputation preceded them. Colourful reports spoke to the exploits of players such as Charlie Bannerman, John Blackman, Dave Gregory and Frederick Spofforth, the fast bowler who was widely referred to as "Fred the Demon". Bannerman, holder of the record for the first century in Australia, struck a match-winning innings of 125 in the game at Montreal, leaving spectators to compare his style and technique to those of none other than W. G. Grace.

Since the visit of the English team in 1859, performance standards in the Canadian game had improved, though not to the same degree as the Australian game over the same period. The Canadians expected to put up a strong showing against the tourists; even though news was widely available within the cricket fraternity of Australia's impressive display in England. As it turned out, the Ontario team of twenty-two, and the Montreal team of the same number, received a thrashing from the Aussies.

The local press did not spare the victims, and condemned their weak performance as a national disgrace. The *Globe*, a newspaper that had distinguished itself for wide coverage of cricket, went on the attack: "Whatever may have been the reasons, however, the fact remains that the Canadian XXII was disastrously defeated by their opponents, and it only remains for Canadians either to give up cricket altogether or in the future avoid such lamentable exhibitions." The link between performance and national pride was now well established, a circumstance that placed tremendous pressure on the players and administrators. At the same time it was recognized that Canadian cricket was presented with a considerable opportunity to show resolve.

The Canadian public was growing restless with respect to the slow climb of the national team to world-beating status. Eager to express itself in the international sport arena the public desired to taste success. When, the following year, another English team arrived to test the national prowess, the public was given nothing to celebrate and little with which to feel confident.

Once again, the Canadians were confronted with a team of English professionals who were handsomely paid by sponsors, and were expected to show value for money on the field. The team was led by Richard Daft, and included Marylebone Cricket Club star players such as Sidney Barnes and Alfred Shaw. Tom Emmett was considered as reliable an English player as could be imagined. The Ontario cricket community played host, and five matches were arranged with district clubs, each fielding a team of twenty-two. The English ruled their opponents royally. Only the presence at the games in Toronto of the vacationing Princess Louise, the queen's daughter, distracted the media from delivering the expected volleys of harsh criticism.

There was, however, an opportunity for some solace later in the year when an Irish team, not rated as a serious contender, arrived to play a number of games in Toronto, Hamilton, Whitby and Cobourg. The Irish were urged to field teams of eleven, matching the Canadians. This arrangement was viewed as part of the national team's preparations for its inaugural tour of England the following year. The Irish won in Toronto and Hamilton but were held to draws at the other venues. This was encouraging, a fitting note on which the Canadians departed for the English challenge.

No dire consequence followed the media's determination to force cricketers to put up, or move out. The number of clubs continued to increase, as did public support. In 1880 the Canadian side toured England, and in 1882 the Edmonton Cricket Club was formed. Two years later officers at Fort Saskatchewan established a cricket club, a signal that while civilians had taken over the game, legacies of its military ancestry remained alive. It was against this background that the West Indian team arrived in Canada.

The West Indians had no international experience and had played no matches against respected figures of the game. They were rookies in every sense, raw and without record. They went on tour to learn the game at the highest level, and if a few commercial contracts could be signed along the way, so much the better. The Canadians were cricketers willing to do business; the West Indians were businessmen looking to enjoy a little cricket. Maybe, just maybe, this is why records of the tour fell off the pages of serious cricket writings for the period.

CRICKET IN THE UNITED STATES IN 1886

The Americans were better at cricket than the Canadians. They had been playing the organized game for a longer period and had invested more in its professional development. They started decades before the modern rules of play were formalized in the 1780s by the English. Even before the English initiated the process of establishing dedicated cricket clubs, immigrants to the American colonies from the English cricketing counties were playing the game in their homesteads. Immigrants imagined the American colonies as "Little Englands", scattered across a vast continent, with a cricket field on every village green.

It was an idyllic picture. On the eve of the Revolutionary War of Independence cricket had become as much a part of the culture of the colonial gentry of Georgia, Maryland and New York as the village parson and tavern. By the end of the century it had found its way into the lifestyles of the intellectual and professional classes, and references to Harvard students exercising at cricket (or wickets as it was oftentimes called), among other sports, are commonplace.[8]

The affluent men of the colonies sent their sons to public schools and universities in England, and expected them to return with the manners and methods of English gentlemen. According to Nancy Struna, "the perception of Englishness was important".[9] The landed elite was prepared to invest heavily in its acquisition. An English gentleman was expected to play "wickets", support the efforts of friends, and so did his colonial counterparts. Mastering the game of "wickets" opened social windows, and with few opportunities available for success in narrow colonial societies, young men took whatever opportunities were considered respectable.

The game of "wickets" figured prominently in the military records of the War of Independence. Officers encouraged their men to play the game as a useful respite from war. According to Bonnie Ledbetter,

> wicket was a form of cricket. Wickets required a long, shovel-shaped bat that was straight on one side and spoon-shaped on the other. The ball was bowled at the wicket that was defended by the player with the bat. If he struck the ball, he had to run to the base of the one who bowled the ball and return to the wicket.[10]

In 1782, after the battle at Valley Forge in Pennsylvania, Lieutenant William

Feltman wrote: "This day I was very much fatigued playing cricket." One soldier wrote a poem to his favourite game:

Camps, hills, and dales with mirth resound;
All with clean clothes and powdered hair
For sport and duty now appear,
Here squad in martial exercise
There whole brigades in order rise.
One Choix of Fives are earned here,
Another furious at Cricket there.[11]

Colonial Anglophiles and officers of the British Army saw to it that cricket remained a part of the American lifestyle even in the heat of war. When hostilities ceased, and the new political leadership took its place at the helm of the victorious nation, cricket remained a celebrated sport largely because it had captured the sporting taste of republicans and royalist alike. "Several of the Founding Fathers of the United States", wrote Deb Das, "were known to be avid cricketers; John Adams among them, who stated in the US Congress in the 1780s that if leaders of cricket clubs could be called 'presidents', there was no reason why the leader of the new nation could not be called the same".[12]

Before the late 1850s, and the subsequent plunge of American society into Civil War over the slavery question, cricket was the principal ball game within the growing white (English) community. The thousands of English immigrants who stepped ashore at New York, for example, brought with them their love of cricket and a loyalty to its place within English culture and identity.

The English were forced to share social space with other European immigrants, such as Germans and Italians, who outnumbered them. This made attachment to their cultural traditions an intense moral and political project. For the twenty-two thousand English inhabitants in Manhattan, for example, out of a population of six hundred thousand in 1855, cricket had no rival. It was the game that allowed them to distinguish themselves from other Europeans whom many considered their cultural inferiors.[13]

Driven by the desire to preserve and politically mobilize "Englishness" for social advantage, English immigrants, and their "creole" admirers, moved to institutionalize cricket as a marker for cultural distinction. The St George's

Society was founded in 1786 with the objective of celebrating all things English, and took as its code respect for royalty and love of cricket. The society created the famous cricket club that bore its name about 1838, providing New Yorkers with the framework within which to promote competitive cricket, featuring engagements with Canadians and English compatriots.

During the 1840s cricket clubs sprung up all over the city promoting the values of the game as the necessary ingredient for manly mental and physical development. Members of the St George's Club toasted visiting cricketers from Philadelphia in 1844 with the following post-dinner jingle:

> With gay men and great
> It is pleasant to meet
> When the Club of St George's may call:
> For true game is there
> All honest and fair;
> 'Tis the game of the Bat and the Ball.[14]

Referring to the advance of cricket among communities along the east coast, the *Atlantic Monthly,* a New York journal, informed readers in 1858 that cricket was everywhere being played, though it noted that baseball was fast gaining ground among the younger generation born on American soil. The *New York Clipper,* another journal, held the brief for cricket and promoted it against the rising claims of baseball. It informed its readers: "We shall feel truly gratified if an amusement of such excellent character shall take firm root in our midst and become, as it already has in England, our chief and most patronized game. We venture to predict", the paper went on to conclude, "that the majority will pronounce it to be the best game played in the open air".[15] The evidence, it seems, was on the *Clipper's* side. When the majestic Central Park was built in 1858, city architects had set aside ten acres of land for the inclusion of cricket facilities.

New York may have given cricket in the United States its early institutional impetus but it was in Philadelphia that it truly flourished, becoming the hub of Englishness with an American style and texture. Elite Philadelphians embraced cricket as a social practice that enabled them to concretize important social distinctions of race and class. To examine the membership list of early clubs in the city is to conduct a tour of the leading families in the dominant public professions. Cricket was associated with class power, and in pre-revolutionary America this meant a great deal for the politics of English cultural norms.

The 1820s was a critical watershed in the development of Philadelphian cricket infrastructures. Driven by a large English immigration the early cricket operations took a shape not dissimilar to what obtained in England. All social classes played the game, and it was not uncommon for "gentlemen and workers" and "locals and immigrants" to play each other. From the 1830s, the Union Cricket Club was aggressive in its promotion of the game as an activity for all classes. At an early stage, then, clubs took on specific class identities that the elite sought to encourage. Class mingling on the field did not spill out beyond the boundary, but it did serve to promote the popularity of the game.

The University of Philadelphia was soon immersed in the politics of the game. Professor John Mitchell was an early advocate of student participation, and the university soon developed a club with dedicated facilities. Meanwhile, as part of the effort at democratization, John Wister, a member of the Union Cricket Club, organized a working men's cricket club among the weavers of neighbouring Germantown. What followed was the establishment of Germantown Cricket Club.

By the 1850, the university team was playing games against the workers in Germantown and other neighbouring communities. In an examination of cricket and social life in Philadelphia, Thomas Jable notes:

> [C]ricketers came from all classes and virtually all sectors of the population including African Americans who organized no less than three cricket clubs in the mid-1860s. The sport, however, did not transcend racial barriers as there are no records of black cricketers playing for or against white clubs. In mid-Victorian Philadelphia, university players were largely middle and upper class, whereas in the neighborhoods the culture was more democratic.[16]

As in the West Indies, the landed elite took command of the institutional leadership of the game. Unlike in the West Indies, however, the local aristocracy was emerging financially secure and politically confident. In 1854, in an act of solidarity, it established the Philadelphia Cricket Club, a major development that gave professional leadership and financial support to the burgeoning cricket culture.

By 1860 Philadelphians were proud of their network of cricket clubs that featured the prestigious Philadelphia Cricket Club and the expanding Germantown Cricket Club. The West Indian community followed this path of institutional formation, suggesting similarities in the development of the cricket culture in the two societies. Minor clubs competed against each other within the city and environs, laying foundations for a vibrant competitive system that called for the widest possible participation.

The Philadelphia Cricket Club took the game beyond city limits and developed both national underpinnings and international operations, which secured for US cricket a place within the global game. The Philadelphia Cricket Club competed with clubs in New York, such as the St George's, and in New Jersey. Occasionally, American clubs joined ranks and played matches across the border in Canada.

The Midwest was not without its cricket in these early years. Tom Melville has shown that cricket clubs could be found, mostly among the immigrant English community, in Ohio, Michigan, Illinois and Indiana. There were several clubs in the small towns of Wisconsin when it was admitted to the Union in 1848 as the thirtieth state. Attracted by the temperate climate, as well as good and relatively inexpensive agricultural land, English immigrants poured into Lisbon in Waukesha County and established the state's first cricket club in 1851. During the remainder of the decade a series of popular matches was organized with players from nearby Milwaukee. In turn, the players from Milwaukee and across Wisconsin came together to compete annually against players from Chicago.[17]

The California gold rush of 1848 pulled to the west coast its share of cricketers and cricket lovers. The trek continued into the 1850s and cricket clubs were among the first institutions that emerged within the English community, particularly in the San Francisco area. By the time the San Francisco Cricket Club was established in March 1852, club matches were a common weekend activity in the town. Historians have now shown that the San Francisco Cricket Club was the "city's first official sporting organization".[18]

Not surprisingly, the first president of the club was the English consul, George Aiken, who took it upon himself to "organize a number of gentlemen in the city" for the purpose of establishing a cricket club whose membership was based on social respectability. Park describes the origins and development of the San Francisco arrangements as follows:

During the 1850s matches were casual and included novelty events such as single wicket contests. Wagering on the outcome was frequent. A pioneer cricket Club was formed in 1857 around the nucleus of the disbanded 1852 group. The California Cricket Club, organized in June of 1857, met at the rooms of the British benevolent Society. Its president was William Lane Booker, HMB Consul; Lane also served as president of the Occident cricket Club, founded in 1874. The San Francisco Cricket Club, organized in 1864, changed its name to the St George Cricket Club in 1868. Other short-lived clubs included the Union Cricket Club and the Excelsior Baseball and Cricket Club. The Olympic club celebrated July 4th, 1882, with a large track meet and a match between the Marions and Occidents.[19]

Cricket, then, had spread like a blanket across the length and breadth of the enormous nation. From east to west, clubs were engaged in organized contests and it could not be denied, the *Clipper* announced in 1856, that cricket was "generally considered the national game among Americans, and right well it deserves that appellation". When the Prince of Wales visited New York in 1860, the *Clipper* welcomed him and took pride in the arrangements that included watching a match of "Our National Game".[20]

By 1850 the Americans were ready to embark upon the international scene. Like the Canadians, they did not look to the West Indies, where they considered the standard inferior, but to the English. The West Indians had no chance of attracting such an international rival. The Americans were bursting with enthusiasm for foreign engagements. Discussion began in 1856 to secure the visit of an English XI to challenge the leading clubs in New York and Philadelphia. Arrangements were finalized the following year, and a team composed mainly of county professionals was assembled for a New York engagement.

The touring party departed from Liverpool on board the *Nova Scotian.* Financial arrangements were settled in the form of a £500 guarantee provided by a Mr Waller, a New Yorker who was a member of the St George's Club, with business interests in England. It was an impressive team of English players, the first of their kind to depart for an overseas tour. Listed within the XI were: Lockyer, Caesar, Stephenson and Caffyn of Surrey; Parr, Jackson and Grundy of Nottinghamshire; Wisden and Lillywhite of Sussex; and Carpenter, Diver and Hayward of Cambridgeshire.

The visitors were given a glorious welcome in New York and New Jersey. The mayors of both cities treated the visiting team to gala dinners, and the media made a great deal of the symbolic nature of the encounter. The *Clipper* promoted the tour and suggested that it was the beginning of the American journey to the finest standard of cricket possible. It was a historic event indeed.

Fittingly, the English party arrived with Fred Lillywhite, known historian of the game, whose mandate was to capture the magical moments of the experience for a curious English cricket public. Lillywhite's "little book of the tour", the first of a plethora of touring literature, has been described as "a classic of the game".[21]

New Jersey, rather than New York, was chosen as the venue for the first contest. A three-day game was played at Hoboken from 3 to 5 October. It was billed as an encounter between England and America, and considered the first international for both countries. The America media hyped the game with several sensational commentaries that appeared in newspapers from New York to Philadelphia.

What ensued was a large gathering of cricket lovers, mostly English immigrants, many of whom were divided in their loyalties with respect to which team to support. The outcome of the game, however, was one-sided. The English professionals demonstrated the enormous performance difference between themselves and the amateurs they played. Scoring 156, the English XI then bowled out the Americans twice, for 38 and 54.

As was the custom of the time, in America and Australia, the winning team was expected to play against a team made up of twenty-two rather than eleven players. The game was played in Philadelphia. More so than the opening match in New Jersey, this game demonstrated the considerable superiority of English cricketers before an American public already feeling insecure with respect to its claim to cricket as a legitimate symbol of national expression.

The English XI bundled out the American XXII for 94 and scored 126 in reply. The American mustered a meagre 60 in the second innings, to which the tourists replied with 29 for 3. The Americans won none of the five matches played. Yet, the evidence was clear that outside of the English context the American game was the most advanced.

The series was significant from another perspective. It was played against the backdrop of pending civil war, and by 1861 cannons rather than cricket balls took over the fields of America. Young men hurled balls of fire at each other rather than those of leather. The fire was not friendly, and cricket paid a dear price during the years of hostility. Marder and Lewis wrote:

> The bitter Civil War that broke out in 1861 between the northern and southern states had many unforeseen results, one of which was to establish baseball beyond all doubt as the national game of the United States. Before the war cricket was an established game and baseball was played more by students and children. The difficulties of getting proper equipment and of marking and maintaining pitches were too great during the 4 years of war; it was easy to throw down 4 bags to mark bases and to play baseball on any ground available. Thousands of soldiers learned the game of baseball during the Civil War. When they returned to civil life the future of baseball was assured. With the ruinous war proceeding in America the attention of English cricket tour organizers turned to Australia.[22]

Reduced in popularity and fallen from pride of place, American cricket soldiered on, pressed by the imperative of maintaining for an elite a traditional cultural context. Cricket leaders took the view that if other European ethnic groups, mostly from Germany, Ireland, France and Italy, wished to express their hostility to English cultural dominance by throwing their support behind baseball, they were free do so. They saw their cultural mission in terms of preserving Anglo-Saxon values in American society, a mandate that took them far beyond the boundary.

For some majority ethnic groups within the white communities, not to play cricket was an expression of American patriotism. It was considered by some a way to break once and for all the cultural dominance the English still held over the young republic. Cricket became immersed deeper within the political battle in which it could not claim any innocence. The chickens had come home to roost, and cricket, on the losing side, returned humbly to its social base. There it became a minority sport played by Anglophiles in a plural society, with baseball commanding mass support.

The loyalists in Philadelphia, especially, stood their ground and refused to be bowled over by the anti-English tide sweeping the nation. They invited many English teams to play within their reduced space, and continued to promote their sport as a game for the "cultured and well bred" as opposed to the "rabble" element that loved the noise and rattle surrounding baseball. The politics of the situation did not lend to the improvement of performance, and the journey to excellence was soon abandoned, though it remained a better quality game than what obtained in the West Indies.

The Philadelphians knew that their backs were against the wall, having lost the mind and heartland of America. An English team toured in 1868, played two games in the city, winning both by considerable margins. The last desperate effort to shore up support and consolidate their elite status was to invite the king of the game, royalty so to speak, the great W. G. Grace, to bless their hallowed grounds. They did so in 1872. Grace toured the towns with an amateur English XI captained by R. A. Fitzgerald. It was to be his first and only visit to the cricket fields of America.

The results of the matches played tell the sorry story of the fall of American cricket. In New York, the St George's Club assembled a team of twenty-two that mustered totals of 68, and 8 for the loss of 11 wickets. At Philadelphia, a team of twenty-two amassed 14 all out, and 68 for the loss of 20 wickets. At Boston the XXII scored 26, and 35 for the loss of 13 wickets. It was against this background of deep despair in American cricket that the West Indians were invited to play in 1886.

As with the Canadians, the American cricket development, both in terms of the organization of fixtures and club formation, was far ahead of what obtained in the West Indies. Greater financial resources were certainly an important factor that accounted for this divergence, but ultimately better organizational dedication and official support in the United States cannot be discounted. But during the 1860s the fortunes of cricket culture in the United States and the West Indies moved in different directions.

The 1860s saw the development of major club structures in the West Indies that produced in 1865 the beginning of annual inter-colonial competitions. West Indies cricket was placed on a footing not yet equal to but evolving towards the standard set by the Canadians and the Americans. The American Civil War, however, produced a scorched-earth effect upon the cricket world. It generated considerable anxiety within the young nation about its cultural identity. A century had passed since a War of Independence had produced the Republic, yet it struggled to produce a distinct cultural expression with indigenous institutions that conferred pride and honour.

Cricket was still essentially an English game, designed and delivered to sustain Englishness. But the war of liberation from English colonialism had resulted in the furtherance of the game, maintaining its status of "national game". This inertia suggested a continuing dependence upon the English sensibility and moral empowerment of Anglophiles. An effect of the Civil War, then, was a deepening of the cultural crisis that haunted the nation-building exercise.

In 1868, when the military aspects of war intensified, the quintessentially English game became increasing politically incorrect. The patriotism of Anglophiles was questioned, and the love of things English considered evidence of a lingering neo-colonial mentality to be ridiculed if not eradicated. The New Yorker George Strong laid bare the cultural dilemma when he wrote in his diary: "[W]e are so young a people that we feel the want of nationality, and delight in whatever asserts our national 'America' existence."[23]

One effect of the search for an authentic national sporting symbolism was a fierce call for cricket teams, especially the "national" team, to be made up of American-born players, thereby generating intense home fan support. Another was the push to ensure the rise of baseball as an indigenous game, and therefore politically preferable to cricket. During the late 1860s, Henry Chadwick, the leading sports writer in New York, was prepared to argue that "cricket was in his estimation superior", but baseball was "just suited to the character of the American people, a manly exercise, moral and physical, for American youth".[24]

The politics of sporting engagement during the Civil War was best articulated in 1868 by Chadwick's own experience, as he shifted loyalties from cricket to baseball:

> I was struck with the idea [he wrote] that baseball was just the game for a national sport for Americans. . . . I have devoted myself to improving and fostering the game in every way I thought likely to promote the main object I had in view, viz.: to assist in building up a national game for the country as much as cricket is for England.[25]

In Philadelphia, more so than New York, ideological pressure exerted on the cricket fraternity drove it to dig deeper in defence of its Englishness. Cricketing Anglophiles reacted with their own assertions and took the game and its institutions even closer to practices considered common on the English green. The war, of course, took young men away from their routine, and by the end of the fighting a new pattern of cultural life had emerged, partly critical of the future of Englishness as a standard for the culturally torn and tortured nation.

The elite did not lie down before the challenge from below. It formed the Young America Cricket Club in order to maintain the interest of the youth, and to sow the seed of a future generation of administrators and players. Despite this strategic initiative, noted Jable, "by the end of the Civil War, a combination of forces made cricket more homogeneous and exclusive, a trend that continued to threaten the social reproduction of the game".

As the game and clubs became increasing elitist, detachment from community life was assured. The number of members and players dwindled, and fewer clubs existed in 1886 than in 1856. Describing the process of decline, Jable notes: "The PCC [Philadelphia Cricket Club] and GCC [Germantown Cricket Club], and the Young America Cricket Club survived the war, but limited resources and diminished playing space forced the consolidation of the PCC with the Chestnut Hill Cricket Club in 1882 and the GCC with Young America seven years later. . . . Joining the PCC and GCC were two new cricket clubs, the Merion and Belmont", located in the suburbs.[26]

These were the surviving clubs that welcomed the West Indians in 1886. They were middle-class institutions with loyal aristocratic support, particularly those with strong business connections in the city. They eagerly anticipated the arrival of the West Indians, largely because they saw in them an example of what they had lost; control over a game that was threatened by the rising tide of mass culture. They looked upon the West Indians as social and political allies; men who had lost their slaves but kept plantations as the key to sustaining much of the old way of life.

SUGAR AND CRICKET: THE TOUR CONCEIVED

The West Indians also had their agenda, which was wider than the physical parameters of the game. It was an opportune time to engage the Canadians and Americans. Not because the quality of their game had advanced to a highly competitive level, but because it was in their business interests to do so. Cricket was in the hands of the sugar interests, whose intention was to bend its culture to serve, in addition to socio-cultural objectives, a precise and focused corporate agenda.

By 1880, the planters were in deep financial and commercial difficulty. The quality of their game had been slowly rising while the same could not be said for their economic fortunes. They needed new business partners and reliable investment opportunities. The Sugar Duties Act, passed in 1846, was having its long-term effects, some of which were of a radical social nature. The colonies might not have seen an American-style civil war, but a series of black rebellions, occasioned by the inequities of the emancipation process, was ripping the "free" societies apart. Workers' rebellions in Guyana in 1856, Jamaica in 1865, and Barbados in 1876, for example, suggest the existence of a kind of West Indian civil war.

The sugar elite faced mounting problems. The region was in dire need of direct foreign investment and new markets. In August 1846 the British prime minister, Lord John Russell, announced that all countries exporting sugar to Britain would pay the same level of sugar duties. This meant that West Indian colonies would have no special treatment as sellers in the British market. The Sugar Duties Act provided that taxes on all foreign sugar would be the same whether it was slave grown or free grown. After 1854 the taxes on all sugar entering the British market were equalized.

This development satisfied European customers who were calling for "free trade", which meant that they wanted the freedom to buy sugar from slave producers, at the best price. The growing of commercial beet sugar crops started in France and then spread across Northern Europe to Belgium, the German states, to Austria-Hungary, Russia and to England. In addition to beet sugar competition, the West Indies had to compete with new producers of cane sugar in Bengal, Mauritius, Reunion, Java, Fiji, Natal, Australia and Hawaii. In the decade up to 1886 they suffered a 25 per cent drop in the sale of their sugar to the British market.

Under these changed circumstances West Indian sugar producers found it difficult to make a profit. Only producers in Hispanic Cuba, and to a lesser extent Puerto Rico, because of their reliance on heavy American and Canadian investments, seemed confident that they could make attractive profits from sugar. The objective of the West Indians was to attract some of this American investment and to open wider the doors for sugar in North America.

There were other disastrous effects of the beginning of free trade. Government found it a challenge to collect taxes because merchant shippers had difficulty selling cargoes and paying customs duties. Money shortages meant the government could not always pay the salaries of public officials or the wages of workers. The result was an industrial relations climate that bred violent conflict.

Members of the West India Committee in London, in their role as supporters of the planters, called for an end to the free trade agenda. The progressive element within the community, knew, however, that a positive response was required. The Americans and Canadian were principal investors in the modernized Cuban and Puerto Rican sugar economy. It was hoped that such investments would travel further south into the British colonies.

The British government did what it was fond of doing in situations of crisis. In 1882 it established a Royal Commission to investigate the state of the West Indian economy. An earlier Select Committee of Enquiry in 1847–1848 had examined the condition of the sugar and coffee industries. Its report did not recommend the need to rely on new sources of "foreign" investments, but noted that planters should take steps to diversify the economy. In 1882 the Royal Commission was sent to Jamaica, the Leeward and the Windward islands. Its aim was to look into new methods of raising investments for the sugar sector.

The report was published in three parts in 1883 and 1884. It emphasized that competition in the British market would increasingly force West Indian producers to look to non-traditional markets, the United States and Canada especially. In 1884 nearly 30 per cent of the total sugar out of the region went to the United States, including 50 per cent of that exported from Trinidad and Guyana.

WEST INDIAN TEAM IN CANADA AND THE UNITED STATES

The West Indians in 1886 ranked beneath the Canadians and Americans in terms of the quality of their game. They were certainly not in the same league as the English and Australians. Their potential was spoken of but no one who followed the international game imagined that they could defeat the mighty Americans. They were in with a chance against the Canadians, whose record against touring teams was weak. But the American clubs, especially teams from Philadelphia, were high-class outfits.

But the tour had many objectives; other considerations motivated the West Indians. Cricket and commerce went bat and glove; this much was understood and appreciated. The outcomes of matches, important in themselves, were not the key determinants in relations between teams. The entire exercise had to be conducted with grace, shaped by hospitality and expressive of gentlemanly conduct. These values were considered endemic to both the culture of the game and commercial ethics.

For the better part of the tour, the weather was fine and well suited to cricket. West Indians were not discomforted by the elements, though slower pitches posed some special challenges. There was reasonable spacing between matches to accommodate travel schedules, social and business engagements. Sightseeing tours were arranged and provided excellent contexts for commercial discussions. Frequent dinner parties served as perfect opportunities to strengthen social bonds.

The tour was the brainchild of Guy Wyatt, captain of the Georgetown Cricket Club in Guyana. It was proposed as an opportunity for "friendly contest" with northern neighbours, and presented in this language to the secretary of the Montreal Cricket Club. Putting together the strongest team was not expected to be an easy matter. Many of the more reliable players had other business engagements. As expected, the original squad was selected from the "Big Four" – Guyana, Jamaica, Trinidad and Barbados, though eventually Trinidad could not send its selected players.

The touring party eventually consisted of seven Jamaicans (L. R. Fyfe, J. Lees, L. Isaacs, W. H. Farquharson, E. N. Marshall, P. Isaacs and J. Burke); three Barbadians (T. S. and E. M. Skeete, and W. O. Collymore) and three Guyanese (G. Wyatt, L. Keer, A. Swain). Fyfe was appointed captain.

. . In all, thirteen matches were played. The West Indies team won six, lost five and two were drawn. It was a fairly mixed sort of tour from the point of view of results. There was a striking disparity in the results between the first leg of the tour in Canada, and the American component that followed. This reflected what seemed possible at the outset. The team performed well in Canada and poorly in the United States.

Six matches were played in Canada; against the Halifax Wanderers, Ottawa Cricket Club, Toronto Cricket Club, Ontario Association XI, Montreal Cricket Club and Hamilton Cricket Club. The West Indians lost one of these matches; it was a heavy defeat by 7 wickets against Hamilton. In so doing, the West Indians presented the Canadians with their first victory in forty-four years over a touring team. West Indians explained the defeat in terms of the "fatigue" that caused the team to "rest" J. M. Burke, its leading bowler. Burke bowled 487 overs on the tour, more than W. H. Farquharson, the senior bowler, by 101. He also took the most wickets on tour: 65 at an average of 10.1 runs compared with Farquharson's 61 wickets at 9.16.

Fortunes were reversed when the team arrived in the United States, where the roots of a professional culture were firmly planted. Two years before the tour the Amateur Athletic Association of Canada was established and became more than evangelical about the preservation of amateurism in cricket, even though they had been clobbered by two generations of English professionals. The Americans had an entirely different approach. The Belmont Cricket Club in Philadelphia, for example, had retained the coaching and playing services of Arthur Wood, the Derbyshire County player, in order to create a young cadre of professionals. His tenure at Belmont was critical in the creation of a Philadelphian approach. According to Cooper:

> The standard of Australian cricketers improved rapidly in the second half of the nineteenth century. On 29 August 1882, the legendary "Ashes" series between England and Australia was born following the surprise Australian victory at the Oval. This victory had its roots in the earlier efforts of English professional coaches Charles Lawrence and William Caffyn, who raised the standard of performance of Australian players between 1860 and 1880. In Canada professionals were seen as outcast by those who were involved in the organization of amateur sport. Canadian cricketers and administrators were some of the most ardent supporters of the amateur philosophy, even though it was to the detriment of their own sport.[27]

The Belmont Cricket Club was home to an oasis of Englishness. Wood was an added, but predictable component within this ideological firmament. J. A. Scott, the captain, not surprisingly, was a "gentleman who hails from the old country". Fyfe's description of a post-game experience sets out the texture of their Anglophile worldview:

> A pleasant incident of this evening occurred at the close, when, on our passing through the club room on our way out of the Pavilion, one of the "Belmonts" sat down at the piano, and played "God save the Queen"; and it is hard to say whether the words of this grand old national song were sung more heartily by us who were subjects of our beloved Queen, than by the body of kindly Americans, who had done so much to make the period of our intercourse with them pass socially and agreeably.

Seven matches were played against the Americans. As expected no matches were won against clubs in Philadelphia. Belmont Cricket Club and Germantown Cricket Club, two of the strongest clubs in America, defeated the West Indians by an innings. No West Indian batsman averaged more than 25 runs on the entire tour; Jack Lees topped the averages with a meagre 22.4, followed by E. N. Marshall with 14.7. Fyfe admitted to the superior standard of American play. On the whole, he wrote, "we had a capital time in Philadelphia and saw some excellent cricket amongst the several clubs. While in many cases the batting of our opponents was of a very high order, the fielding, especially of the Belmont's and the Germantown's, could scarcely be surpassed."

The *Philadelphia Times* of 4 September described the West Indians as offering "a somewhat indifferent showing", being defeated by "a rather weak eleven" by 10 wickets. In the match against the Belmont Cricket Club "they were compelled to hunt leather for many long hours", and local opinion suggests that no one should be surprised by their "poor work against the strong organizations" they met in Philadelphia.

The match against the Young America Cricket Club at Stenton, Philadelphia, was played on 7 and 8 September. It almost ended in disaster for the West Indians, who held on to a draw after trailing on first innings by 195. The result was described as a "slight concession" to the West Indians, which "filled them with pride". The game was played before a small crowd mainly of "carriage parties, who, after a brief stay, and upon hearing that the Young American men were doing quite well, drove to other and more interesting pursuits". The West Indians, as a result, departed Philadelphia in considerable doubt about their standard of play, wondering if they could ever match the cricketing abilities of the Americans.

Sections of the American press sympathized with the West Indians and explained their poor performance in terms of specific circumstances of the tour. One journalist noted:

> The islanders are not accustomed to American wickets, their own being harder, rougher and faster. Again, they are under too great a strain. They play cricket day after day, and generally spend their evening in enjoying the hospitality of their hosts. These are the principal reasons why they have failed to do themselves justice.

In general, cricket journalists cast rather harsh judgment on the overall West Indian standard of cricket. The *Philadelphia Times,* offering an analysis of the touring party, noted their limitations:

> Generally speaking, however, the team is deficient in bowling talent, and were it not

for good, steady fielding, the scores against them would be larger than they are. To sum up, the visitors are playing under many disadvantages, but, making every allowance possible, it is clear that they are not up to the form of the leading local clubs.

The West Indians, then, on their first overseas tour to the United States, were made to feel quite inferior. Captain Fyfe, in his account of the tour, however, painted a less grim picture. In the first instance, he noted, many West Indians considered the proposed tour a "farce". Despite being "sneered and laughed at by many more than most people imagine", the team was able to experience the demanding rigour of an overseas tour. The outcome, he noted, was a lasting experience that augured well for West Indies cricket. It was not the strongest West Indies team, noted Fyfe, though it might very well have been the wealthiest. The entire cost of the tour amounted to "near £1,000", an average of £71 or $340 per man for nine weeks. The cost for players from Guyana and Barbados amounted to more than that for the Jamaicans on account of the shorter journey of the latter.

The West Indians had followed the English into North America. They had not done as well, but were looking forward to an exciting future. Fyfe concluded:

> The ball has been set a-rolling now, and if the result of our recent tour gives us many visits in the West Indies from our Canadian and American friends, and wakes up our Island neighbours and our own Colony to move about amongst each other and further afield, in the interest of the noble game, something tangible and well worth having will have been gained, and the writer fully and well recompensed for what trouble he has taken in the matter. But a hint to our island neighbours must be given. Some proper and really strong move must be made to secure permanent and good cricket grounds everywhere in the West Indies where the game is to take any standing, and let us hope that nowhere will this latter not be the case. In Barbados especially, the rendezvous and headquarters for all passenger steamers, there ought certainly to be the best ground in the West Indies, and we trust that the "blot" (for such it is) of not having such a ground will not continue much longer.

The following year the Americans returned the visit, but played against territorial sides rather than a West Indies team. It was a weak team and was defeated by Trinidad, Guyana, Jamaica and Barbados. The Barbados and Jamaica matches were billed as "America vs Barbados" and "Gentlemen of

America vs All-Jamaica" respectively. By this time the writing was on the wall for American cricket. The Civil War had ravaged the national game, leaving it a poor third to baseball and football.

Notes

1. Robert Lewis, "Cricket and the Beginnings of Organized Baseball in New York City", *International Journal of the History of Sport* 4 (December 1987).
2. Jon Harris, "Cricket in Canada: A Historical Review", http://www.cricketeurope.org (May 2001).
3. Deb K. Das, "Cricket in America", *Cricketer International's North American Edition* (1994).
4. Kenneth R. Bullock, "Canada", in *Barclay's World of Cricket*, ed. by E.W. Swanton (London: Collins, 1980).
5. Hilary McD. Beckles, *The Development of West Indies Cricket*, vol. 1, *The Age of Nationalism;* vol. 2, *The Age of Globalization* (Kingston: University of the West Indies Press, 1999).
6. Bullock, "Canada".
7. Ibid.
8. John Betts, "Mind and Body in Early American Thought", *Journal of American History* 54 (1968): 795.
9. Nancy Struna, "The Formalizing of Sport and the Formation of an Elite: The Chesapeake Gentry, 1650–1720", *Journal of Sport History* 13, no. 3 (Winter 1986): 230.
10. Bonnie Ledbetter, "Sports and Games of the American Revolution", *Journal of Sports History* 6, no. 3 (Winter 1979): 30–31.
11. Ibid., 31.
12. Das, "Cricket in America".
13. Lewis, "Cricket and the Beginnings of Organized Baseball", 321.
14. Ibid., 323.
15. Ibid., 317.
16. John T. Jable, "Social Class and the Sport of Cricket in Philadelphia, 1850–1880", *Journal of Sport History* 18, no. 2 (Summer 1991): 214–15.
17. Tom Melville, "*De Gustibus non est Disputandum:* Cricket at St Paul's School and a Note on the Structural/Character Debate in American Cricket", *International Journal of the History of Sport* 9, no. 1 (April 1992): 281.
18. Roberta Park, "British Sports and Pastimes in San Francisco, 1848–1900", *British Journal of Sports History* 1, no. 3 (1984): 304.
19. Ibid.

20. Lewis, "Cricket and the Beginnings of Organized Baseball", 327.
21. John Marder and Vic Lewis, "America", in *Barclay's World of Cricket*, ed. E. W. Swanton (London: Collins, 1980), 127.
22. Ibid.
23. Lewis, "Cricket and the Beginnings of Organized Baseball", 327.
24. Ibid., 328.
25. Ibid.
26. Jable, "Social Class", 218.
27. David Cooper, "Canadians Declare 'It Isn't Cricket': A Century of Rejection of the Imperial Game, 1860–1960", *Journal of Sport History* 26, no. 1 (1999): 75.

Bibliography

Adelman, Melvin L. *A Sporting Time.* Urban: University of Illinois Press, 1986.

Baker, William. "Disputed Diamonds: The YMCA Debate over Baseball in the Late Nineteenth Century". *Journal of Sport History* 19, no. 3 (1992).

Batts, John S. "Cricket and the British Sporting Ethic of Victorian Canada". Paper presented at HISPA: Sixth International Congress, International Association for History of Physical Education and Sport. Dartford, England, 11–16 April 1977.

Beckles, Hilary. *The Development of West Indies Cricket*, vol. 1, *The Age of Nationalism;* vol. 2, *The Age of Globalization.* Kingston: University of the West Indies Press, 1999.

———. *A Nation Imagined: First West Indies Test Team – The 1928 Tour.* Kingston: Ian Randle, 2003.

Betts, John. "Mind and Body in Early American Thought". *Journal of American History* 54 (1968).

———. "Sporting Journalism in Nineteenth Century America". *American Quarterly* (Spring 1953).

Boller, Kevin E. "John Ross Robertson Trophy: Symbol of Cricket". *Canadian Cricketer* 22 (1994).

Bouchier, Nancy. "Aristocrats and their Noble Sport: Woodstock Officers and Cricket During the Rebellion Era". *Canadian Journal of History of Sports and Physical Education* 20 (1989).

Bradley, James. "Inventing Australians and Constructing Englishness: Cricket and the Creation of National Consciousness, 1860–1914". *Sporting Traditions* 11 (May 1995).

Brown, David. "Canadian Imperialism and Sporting Exchanges: The Nineteenth-Century Cultural Experience of Cricket and Lacrosse". *Canadian Journal of History of Sports* 18 (May 1987).

Brown, John L. "Canada's Place in Cricket". *National Home Monthly*, July 1937.

Bullock, Kenneth R. "Canada". In *Barclay's World of Cricket*, edited by E.W. Swanton. London: Collins, 1980.

Cooper, David. "Canadians Declare 'It Isn't Cricket': A Century of Rejection of the Imperial Game, 1860–1960". *Journal of Sport History* 26, no. 1 (1999).

———. "Canadians Declare 'It Isn't Cricket': A Colonial Rejection of the Imperial Game". Master's thesis, University of Toronto, 1995.

Crockett, David S. "Sports and Recreational Practices of Union and Confederate Soldiers". *Research Quarterly* 32, no. 3 (1962).

Das, Deb K. "Cricket in America". *Cricketer International's North American Edition*, 1994.

Fitzgerald, R. A. *Wickets in the West, Or the Twelve in America*. Tinsley, 1873.

Gelber, Steven. "Their Hands Are All Out Playing: Business and Amateur Baseball, 1845–1917". *Journal of Sport History* 11, no. 1 (Spring 1984).

Hall, John E., and Robert O. McCulloch. *Sixty Years of Canadian Cricket*. Toronto: Bryant, 1895.

Harris, Jon. "Cricket in Canada: A Historical Review". http://www.cricketeurope.org. May 2001.

Harte, Chris. *A History of Australian Cricket*. London: Deutsch, 1993.

Jable, John T. "Latter-Day Culture Imperialists: The British Influence on the Establishment of Cricket in Philadelphia, 1842–72". In *Pleasure, Profit, Proselytism: British Culture and Sports at Home and Abroad 1700–1914*, edited by J.A. Mangan. London: Frank Cass, 1988.

———. "Social Class and the Sport of Cricket in Philadelphia, 1850–1880". *Journal of Sport History* 18, no. 2 (Summer 1991).

Jarvie, Grant, ed. *Sport, Racism and Ethnicity*. London: Falmer, 1991.

Kirsch, George B. *The Creation of American Team Sports*. Urbana: University of Illinois Press, 1986.

Ledbetter, Bonnie. "Sports and Games of the American Revolution". *Journal of Sports History* 6, no. 3 (Winter 1979).

Lewis, Robert. "Cricket and the Beginnings of Organized Baseball in New York City". *International Journal of the History of Sport* 4 (December 1987).

Lindsay, Peter. "The Impact of Military Garrison on the Development of Sport in British North America". *Canadian Journal of History and Sport and Physical Education* 1 (May 1970).

Maguire, Joe. "More Than a Sporting Touchdown: The Making of American Football in England, 1982–1990". *Sociology of Sports Journal* 7 (September 1990).

Mandle, William F. "Cricket and Australian Nationalism in the Nineteenth Century". *Journal of the Royal Australian Historical Society* 59 (December 1973).

———. "The Professional Cricketer in England in the Nineteenth Century". *Labour History* 23 (1972).

Mangan, J. A. *The Game Ethic and Imperialism*. Harmondsworth: Penguin, 1986.

————, ed. "Eton in India: The Imperial Diffusion of a Victorian Education Ethic". *History of Education* 7 (1978).

————. *Pleasure, Profit, Proselytism: British Culture and Sports at Home and Abroad 1700–1914*. London: Frank Cass, 1988.

Marder, John, and Vic Lewis. "America". In *Barclay's World of Cricket,* edited by E.W. Swanton. London: Collins, 1980.

Melville, Tom. "*De Gustibus non est Disputandum:* Cricket at St Paul's School and a Note on the Structural/Character Debate in American Cricket". *International Journal of the History of Sport* 9, no. 1 (April 1992).

————. "From Ethnic Tradition to Community Institution: Nineteenth-Century Cricket in Small Town Wisconsin and a Note on the Enigma of a Sporting Discontinuity". *International Journal of the History of Sport* 11, no. 2 (August 1994).

————. *The Tented Field: A History of Cricket in America*. Bowling Green: Bowling Green State University, 1988.

Metcalfe, Alan. *Canada Learns to Play.* Toronto: McClelland and Stewart, 1987.

Park, Roberta. "British Sports and Pastimes in San Francisco, 1848–1900". *British Journal of Sports History* 1, no. 3 (1984).

Pesavento, Wilma. " 'Men Must Play, Men Will Play': Occupations of Pullman Athletes, 1880 to 1900". *Journal of Sport History* 12, no. 3 (Winter 1985).

Pridham, C. H. B. *The Charm of Cricket Past and Present.* Herbert Jenkins, 1949.

Rader, Hilary. "The Quest for Sub-Communities and the Rise of American Sport". *American Quarterly* 29 (1977).

Redmond, Gerald. "Imperial Vice-Regal Patronage: The Governors-General of Canada and Sport in the Dominion, 1867–1909". *International Journal of History of Sport* 6 (September 1989).

Sandiford, Keith. *Cricket and the Victorians.* Aldershot, UK: Scolar Press, 1994.

Scott, Patrick. "Cricket and the Religious World in the Victorian Period". *Church Quarterly* 3, no. 2 (October 1970).

Stoddart, Brian. "Cricket and Colonialism in the English Speaking Caribbean to 1914: Towards a Cultural Analysis". In *Pleasure, Profit, Proselytism: British Culture and Sport at Home and Abroad, 1700–1914,* edited by J.A. Mangan. London: Frank Cass, 1988.

Stout, Neil. "1874 Baseball Tour Not Cricket to British". *Baseball Research Journal* 14 (1985).

Struna, Nancy. "The Formalizing of Sport and the Formation of an Elite: The Chesapeake Gentry, 1650–1720". *Journal of Sport History* 13, no. 3 (Winter 1986).

Tyrell, Ian. "The Emergence of Modern American Baseball, c.1850–1880". In *Sport in History,* edited by Richard Cashman and Michael Mckernan, 205–26. Queensland: University of Queensland Press, 1979.

Whiting, Cohn. *Cricket in Eastern Canada.* Montreal: Colmur, 1963.

Winn, William. "Tom Brown's Schooldays and the Development of 'Muscular Christianity' ". *Church History* 21 (1960).

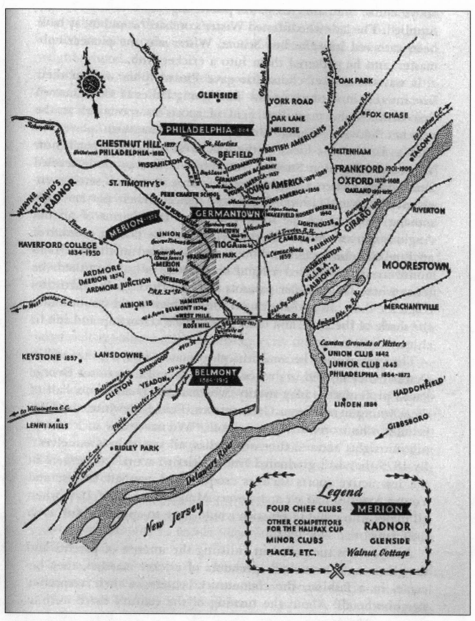

Map of Philadelphia clubs

Sketch of the US–Canada match at Hoboken, 1856

English cricket team that toured North America in 1859 (Captain George Parr standing middle of back row)

Cricket in the park, Montreal, *c*.1870

Sketch of the match between Australia and Philadelphia, Nicetown, Pennsylvania, 1878

The Paterson Cricket Club members, New Jersey, 1880

Belmont Cricket Club, Philadelphia, *c.*1890

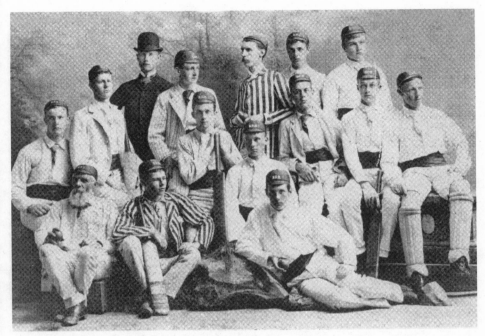

The St Paul's school cricket team, New Hampshire, *c.*1890

Cricket in the park, Toronto, *c.*1891

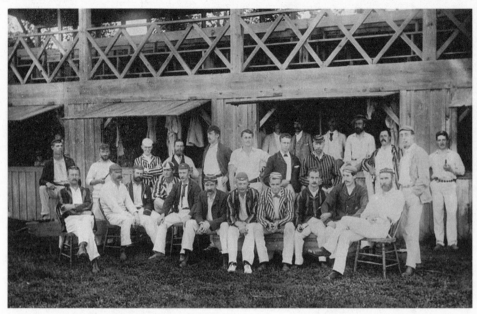

Ottawa cricket team, August 1891

Halifax cricket team, *c.*1895

Hazen School girls' cricket team, Pelham, New York, 1896

Ottawa cricket team, July 1898

West Indians versus Germantown Club at Nicetown, Pennsylvania, 1886 (engraving). *Harper's Weekly*, 25 September 1886.

Cope Field at Haverford College

The Tour

of the

West Indian Cricketers

———

August & September, 1886

———

THE "ARGOSY" PRESS, DEMERARA
1887

The Tour of the West Indian Cricketers

August & September, 1886

"A MEMORY."

By One of Them.

The idea of collecting a team of cricketers from the several West Indian Colonies to visit the United States and Canada, for the purpose of playing a series of matches with such of the Clubs as would be ready to engage in friendly contest with them, was originated by Mr. Guy Wyatt, the Captain of the Georgetown C. C. of Demerara, and he first put his idea into practical shape in a letter which he addressed to Mr. Dean, the Secretary of the Montreal C. C., on the 28th of Sept., 1885.

The suggestion for a visit of West Indian cricketers met with a most cordial response in Canada, and it was not long before a programme of fixtures for the West Indian Team was arranged through the kind intervention of the Montreal C. C.

But it was only after considerable correspondence, and in the face of many difficulties and disappointments, that arrangements were finally conducted for the visit of the West Indian Team.

The team as originally proposed differed considerably from that which actually in the end represented the West Indies, and it was a most unfortunate circumstance that such excellent cricketers as Messrs. E. F. Wright, P. J. T.

Henery, A. J. Goodridge, and R. Garnett, of Demerara, were unable to take their places in the team, which was tremendously weakened by their absence.

It has been arranged that the contingents from Demerara and Barbados (the only Colonies besides Jamaica sending representations) should call at Jamaica in order that the team might play some matches together before meeting their powerful antagonists on the other side of the water; but unfortunately, it was at the last moment found impossible to carry out the arrangement, in consequence of the absence of steam ship passage accommodation in Jamaica, at the time it was required.

It therefore became necessary that each of the contingents from the several colonies should find its way to the American Continent irrespective of the others.

The Jamaica Contingent comprised Messrs. L. R. Fyfe, J. Lees, L. Isaacs, W. H. Farquharson, E. N. Marshall, P. Isaacs, J. M. Burke.

They left Port Morant, Jamaica, on the s.s. *L. D. Baker* at midnight, on the 31st July, 1886, and after a pleasant passage landed at Boston on the morning of the 9th of August.

As the first match was fixed to take place at Montreal on the 16th of August, the Jamaicans had some days at their disposal, which they devoted to the pleasures of sight, and to steady practice in the afternoons, which latter they were able to obtain by the courtesy of the Longwood C. C. who kindly placed their ground at the disposal of the Jamaicans during their stay in Boston. The Jamaicans were no less impressed with the business-like bustle of Boston and with its splendid buildings, than charmed with the beauty of its suburbs; and it was with no small feeling of regret that they felt compelled to quit so much that was agreeable and pleasant on their way to the North. They left Boston on the morning of Thursday, the 12th August, and arrived at Montreal the same evening. They were met at the station by Mr. Thomas Trimble, secretary of the Montreal C. C., and Mr. Short of the same club. Mr. Trimble thus inaugurated a series of courtesies and attentions to the West Indian cricketers which continued throughout their stay in Montreal and which will ever be gratefully remembered. Through the courtesy and kindness of Mr. Macaulay of the Sun Life Assurance Society of Montreal (a representative of which we had with us in the person of Mr. W. Hussy Fyfe), the cricketers were taken on Friday morning for a drive up "the mountain", from which a magnificent view of Montreal and its surroundings was enjoyed, and on the following morning under the same kind auspices the "Lachine rapids" were shot. On the evening of the same day, the Jamaica cricketers were guests at the banquet given at the Windsor Hotel by the Montreal Lacrosse Club to the team of Lacrosse players from Ireland; they have pleasant recollections of the kind terms in which their health was proposed by the worthy President of the Club, and the equally kind manner in which it was received by the large company of lacrosse players present.

Mr. Fyfe, on behalf of the Cricketers, said a few suitable words of thanks for the honour conferred. A copy of the Ménu is appended. If it serves no other purpose it will recall a gastronomic treat to those who were fortunate enough to partake of the dinner.

MENU.

Soup.—Green turtle. Consommé Royal.

Fish.—Boiled chicken halibut; cream sauce. Pommes Parisienne. White fish; Hollandaise sauce; cucumbers.

Réléves.—Roast beef. Spring duck; apple jelly.

Vegetables.—Cauliflower. Green peas. Vegetable marrows. Tomatoes.

Entrées.—Filet of beef larded with mushrooms, Spring chicken. Sauté Marengo. Soft shell crabs. Maitre d'Hôtel. Sorbet Windsor. Broiled squabs. Lettuce salad.

Dessert.—Glace Napolitaine. Ice cream. Champagne jelly. Gateau Juisse. Fruits. Coffee.

It was on this evening that we first made acquaintance with two "ways of the country" which were certainly new to us.

On the mention of any name, to which it was desired to give a popular reception, the cry would go up from some stentorian voice "What's the matter with ———?" Then the answer would come as with one voice from the whole assemblage, "Oh! He's all right; oh yes, oh yes." The second custom alluded to was that of "bouncing." It is considered a high honour to be "bounced"; the individual on whom this honour is to be conferred is suddenly seized by stalwart arms and tossed high in the air and then skilfully caught in his descent. It would be sudden death evidently if the "bounced" one were allowed to fall; but it was said that this was never known to happen, and certainly the skilful manner in which the "evergreen" skipper (who was not at all happy during the operation) was "bounced" seemed to justify this statement.

In the meantime, the Jamaica cricketers could get no tidings of their companions from Demerara and Barbados. All they knew was that the Demerara contingent had arrived at Barbados before they left Jamaica and were to leave that place for New York on the 3rd of August; and up to the evening of Friday the 13th of August, they had received no further news of them. But on Saturday the 14th, a telegram was received from Mr. Wyatt from St. Croix, saying that they would not arrive at New York until the 19th of August.

This was disappointing news, in view of the fact that on Monday the 16th, the first match of the tour against the Montreal C. C. was to be played. To them the detention was aggravating in the extreme, and they afterwards keenly felt the loss of the four jolly days in Montreal. There was no alternative but to play three substitutes; the seven from Jamaica having at the last moment been increased to eight by the arrival from England of Mr. Stewart, one of the Demerara contingent.

Fortunately, three substitutes were readily available in the persons of Mr. Jenoure, of Jamaica, Mr. Austin, of Chamblay, near Montreal (a good fellow whom the West Indian Cricketers hope to meet again), and Mr. Annand, of the "Halifax Wanderers."

As full particulars of the matches are given elsewhere in this pamphlet, it is not proposed to make any but casual references on special points in regard to the matches in this narrative.

The Jamaica cricketers carry most pleasant reminiscences of their match against the Montreal C. C., in which they met some of the pleasantest of cricketers and gentlemen amongst their opponents, headed by the Captain, Mr. Gough—and they feel that this record will not be sufficient without a special reference to the genial and gentlemanly President of the club, Mr. Stancliffe, to whom most warm acknowledgments are due for courtesies and attentions constantly shewn. And mention of Mr. Stancliffe would not be complete without allusion to his charming wife and niece, who spoke many pleasant words of welcome and encouragement to the West Indian cricketers. This part of the narrative methinks will not be altogether without interest to our "gallant son of Mars," whom it proved very difficult to tear from Montreal, for reasons which he doubtless will be able readily to explain.

Through the courtesy of the Montreal C. C. it had been arranged that on the 18th and 19th August, a match between the West Indian Cricketers and the Halifax Wanderers, a powerful club, hailing from Halifax, and the champion club of the Maritime Provinces, should be played on the ground of the Montreal C. C.

As the West Indians were still three men short it was necessary again to play with 3 substitutes, and the services of Mr. Austin (a second time), Mr. B. T. A. Bell, and Mr. James Smith (both of the Montreal C. C.) were secured by Mr. Fyfe. Lovely cricketing weather prevailed throughout the two days, and the West Indians were in great form with the bat. It was remarkable how uniformly well the Halifax Wanderers fielded during the long innings of their opponents. They seemed quite as fresh and active in the last over as they were in the first.

On the morning of the 19th August the contingents from Demerara and Barbados at last arrived at Montreal, so that the West Indian Cricketers were enabled to put a complete team in the field for the first time at Ottawa on the 20th August.

The two contingents consisted of the following gentlemen:— Messrs. G. Wyatt, L. Kerr and A. Swain from Demerara, and Messrs. T. S. and E. M. Skeete and W. O. Collymore from Barbados.

As the West Indians thus became a united party, it will be more convenient to continue this narrative in the first person; and before saying farewell to Montreal it is right to say that we feel that we owe a debt of gratitude for unostentatious kindness tendered to us which we can never repay, whilst we have recollection of pleasant intercourse with the best of fellows and cricketers which will never fade from our memory. Truly we West Indian Cricketers all bade farewell to Montreal with very great regret; and the last notes of "Auld Lang Syne" which were sung hand in hand with so many of the friends we had made in the dear old town, who had come to the station to bid us God-speed, haunted us for many a day in our subsequent travels. We left Montreal for Ottawa on Thursday evening, the 19th August, and arrived at the latter place at about midnight. We were met at the station by Mr. Coste, the Captain of the Ottawa C. C.

Mr. Coste affords, we believe, one of the few instances in which a Frenchman has taken to the game of Cricket and become proficient in it. Mr. Coste escorted us to the "Russell House Hotel," where we were most comfortably located. On the following morning at about 10.30 we started for the Cricket ground, which is a portion of the grounds of Rideau Hall, the residence of the Governor-General of Canada. The ground is most beautifully situated, having the Mansion of Rideau Hall facing the Pavilion. The pitch was thoroughly true, but the wicket was very slow after our hard and fast wickets in the West Indies.

The match was a very pleasant one, and it was charming to meet a lady who knew the game so thoroughly in all its points as did the fair wife of the Captain of the Club. There was another comely lady in whom young "Leo" evidently discovered powers of conversation (whether on cricket topics or others, I know not) which made him oblivious of time and place, whilst our gallant young Kerr was on the verge of being made a "vert" by a fascinating young Roman Catholic lady.

A portion of the luncheon interval was spent in walking through the Rideau Hall Mansion, and the grounds around the house. The tobogganing slides were objects of considerable interest to us.

On the evening of Friday (the first day of the match), we were entertained by the Ottawa C. C., at a banquet at the Russell House. The dinner (of which the menu is given below) was a masterpiece of culinary art; and excellent as it was in itself, it was rendered doubly enjoyable by the genial manner in which it was presided over by the veteran and popular president of the Club, Mr. W. Powell, Under Secretary of State.

MENU.

Petit Neck Clams sur Escailles. Chablis.

Potage.—Consommé de Volaille à la Printaniere Royale. Amontillado Sherry.

Hors D'Oeuvres.—Bouchées à la Mazarin; Olives d'Espagne; Sardines de l'Orient; Pommes Chateaux. Amontillado Sherry.

Entrées.—Pigeon á la Crapaudine; Ris de Veau aux Petits Pois; Amourettes d'Agneaux, Sauces, Pomme d'Amom, B. and G. Sparkling Hock.

Rélevé.—Dinde à la Purée de Celeri. Pommery.

Sorbet.—Framboises à la Démocratique.

Roti.—Filet de boeuf à la Renaissance; Pommes de Terre. Pommery.

Mayonnaise.—Macédoines. Burgundy.

Entremets.—Omelettes aux Rheim: Plum Pudding, Sauce Martel; Gelée de Champagne aux Fruits; Petit Fours Mélés; Charlotte Russe à la Vanille; Gelée au Cognac; Glace Napolitaine. Burgundy.

Dessert.—Melons, Grapes, Apples, Delesa Raisins, Grenoble Walnuts. Claret. Filberts, Almonds, Cheese, Celery, Biscuits. Port wine; Café Noir.

After breakfast on the following morning, Mr. Powell kindly conducted us over the Houses of Parliament and the Public Buildings; they are buildings of great architectural beauty; and the library is especially worthy of a visit, both for the chasteness and variety of its wood work, and for the numbers and valuable character of the works it contains. The grounds round the Houses of Parliament are beautifully laid out and kept, and a charming view of the surrounding scenery is to be obtained both from the Tower over the Parliament Houses, and from a sort of summer house, at the end of one of the walks.

We paid a visit to some of the saw-mills at Ottawa, in which we saw the log as brought from the forest, pass through all its stages, until it was converted into planks and battens, all by water power, and also the electric light battery station which was worked by the same motive power. Our warm acknowledgments are due to Mr. Coste, the captain of the club, for his constant attention to us during our pleasant stay at Ottawa.

We left Ottawa at about mid-night of Saturday the 21st of August, and the train was timed to arrive at Toronto at about 9 the next morning, but owing to a collision having taken place on the line ahead of our train between two freight trains, we were obliged to wait for several hours at a little station named "Mountain Grove," whilst the wreckage was being removed from the line. We did not arrive at Toronto until about 3 o'clock in the afternoon. Here we were met by Mr. Lindsey, the Hon. Secretary of the Toronto Cricket Club, Mr. Winslow, Mr. Perry and other members of the Club.

The next day saw the commencement of the first of our two matches at Toronto, that against the Toronto C. C.

The Club ground is a very picturesque one, having at one end large handsome trees affording excellent shade for spectators, whilst at a little distance in the other direction are seen the handsome buildings of the Toronto University. Both the match against the Toronto C. C. and that against the Ontario Association were much enjoyed by us. We met on the Cricket field at Toronto many excellent fellows to whom we were exceedingly sorry to say "good-bye." During our stay at Toronto the members of the Club were kind enough to take us for a moonlight trip across the bay, to a place called "The Island"—on which, *inter alia*, stands Hanlan's Hotel, which was presented to the great oarsman as the result of subscriptions raised by admirers in Toronto. In one of the rooms of this hotel are presented to public view all the trophies which Hanlan has won, and the presents which have been made to him up to the time of our visit.

It is certainly a wonderful collection. Close to the Hotel we made acquaintance with the "Switch-back"—which is the nearest approach to be obtained to the sensation of going on a toboggan slide; and with the Roller-Coaster railway, "up and down" circular trains traveling with tremendous velocity. One's first experience of these strange means of amusement certainly suggested elements of danger. Indeed, so much was this the case, that some of the older ones, notable the "old salt" and the "evergreen skipper", wished to avoid a second journey on their rapid going cars; but the Toronto men (headed by the genial "Bull" Behan) were not to be denied, and these veterans had to look as if they enjoyed it as thoroughly as did "the Lieutenant," "Papa Wyatt," "Tiny," and the other youngsters. We all went on the "roundabouts" to help to carry us back to the days of our youth.

Having done all the sights of Hanlan's Point, we were taken to the Yacht Club House, where we were received by that most pleasant of gentlemen Mr. Townshend, the President of the Toronto C. C. We supped here as guests of the Toronto C. C. and passed a most enjoyable evening.

The worthy President proved a host in himself, and he was most ably supported by another right good fellow, Dr. Baynes, the Vice-President of the Club, whose handsome and pleasant face was always a welcome sight to us on the Cricket field. We received further courtesies from Mr. Townshend during our stay in Toronto; and our acknowledgments are also due to the jolly President of the Ontario Cricket Association, Mr. Charlton Jones, for bountiful hospitality extended to many of us. This brief record of our visit to Toronto will not be complete without allusion to one of its brightest features, namely, the gathering for afternoon tea, after the Match against the Association was concluded, at the house of the parents of Mr. Vickers, whom we had the pleasure of meeting as a friendly and formidable opponent in both our matches at Toronto. We swooped down upon the pleasant homestead in full numbers; and borne in our memory for many a day will be the kindly welcome and delicious fare of choicest fruits and cakes and ices which we enjoyed on that bright afternoon when a charming mother and charming daughters vied with each other in their efforts to make us bright and happy. Before taking leave of Toronto we cannot avoid a special reference to our pleasant intercourse with that excellent cricketer, Mr. Saunders (the captain of the Toronto Eleven), and the popular secretary of the club, Mr. Lindsey. On the morning of Friday the [27th], we left Toronto for Hamilton. We were met at the station by Mr. Stinton, the popular and ubiquitous secretary of the club. We suffered our first defeat at Hamilton. There can be [no] doubt that we were a good deal worn out with the fatigues of all we had previously undergone, and it became necessary to rest one of our bowlers, Mr. Burke, who had in previous matches done such excellent service with the ball. On the other hand the bowling of Messrs. Gillespie and Ferrie was above the average; and the Hamilton team played up well together and won a good game. We had a larg[er] number of spectators at Hamilton than we had seen in any of our previous matches, and they seemed to follow the game with considerable interest and appreciation of the good points in it.

On the evening of Friday, the first day of our match, we were entertained at dinner at the Hamilton Club by the members of the Hamilton C. C. A most excellent dinner (of which the Menu is given below) was enjoyed, and a very pleasant evening was passed.

MENU.

Oysters.
Soup.—Consommé with egg, à la Reine.
Fish.—Boiled Sea Salmon, lobster sauce. Fillets of White, Mâitre d'Hôtel.
Entrées.—Deviled kidneys with Champignons. Fricassée of sweetbreads. Lamb cutlet with green peas.
Réléves.—Boiled: ———. Roast: Sirloin of beef. Spring lamb, mint sauce. Chicken with ham.
Rots.—Pigeon.
Entremets.—Chancellor's pudding. Lemon Charlotte Russe. Macédoine of fruits. Maraschino jelly.
Cheese.—Stilton. Celery.

The dinner was presided over by the jolly captain of the club, Mr. Kennedy; and pleasant associations in connection with this dinner are mingled with the names of Mr. Stinson, the secretary, Mr. Mackelchan (who makes a good speech and sings a good song), Mr. Stewart and Mr. Bob "Hope." "Bob Hope" is to be remembered for bringing about an innovation which brought great comfort to us. The night was a terribly hot one; and the lively Bob could stand it no longer, so he proposed that we should all take off our coats and finish our dinner in our short sleeves. The president consented, and although the club waiters seemed a little shocked at this outrage on the proprieties of the institution, the change was greatly appreciated by us all.

On the following evening a small dance was given by Mrs. Bruce in honour of our cricketers, and those of us who were able to available themselves of this hospitable lady's kindness, enjoyed themselves thoroughly. Many of us have also words of acknowledgment to offer to Messrs. Henry, Stewart, and Mackelchan for attentions shewn whilst in Hamilton.

On [Sunday], at 10 o'clock, we started for the Niagara Falls, where we arrived at about 2.30. We visited all the points of interest, and were much impressed with the marvelous grandeur of all we saw. But the "fifty-cents' admission" at every turn off proved a stumbling-block to our progress; and I think we were also duly impressed with the marvelous rapidity with which our "dollars" vanished on that memorable afternoon.

Our next move was to the great centre of cricket in the American continent, viz.: Philadelphia. We left Niagara at 8.30 on Monday morning, the 30th August, and arrived at Philadelphia at 11.30 the same night. The journey was a long one, but the beautiful scenery through which we passed rendered it less tedious than it otherwise might have been. Representatives of the different clubs which we were to meet at Philadelphia kindly met us on our arrival at the Colonnade Hotel, and made arrangements for our future movements whilst in the city. Our first match was against the "Merion C. C." and on Tuesday we went by train to "Ardmore" (a few minutes' drive from Philadelphia), near which station the ground is situated. The ground of the "Merion" Club is prettily situated and is kept in excellent order. It is as good in the out-field as at the pitch; and it was a real pleasure to us to play on such a ground. We had two very enjoyable matches against the "Merions", for after they had defeated us early on the second day in our first match, they suggested our playing a second match of an innings each, which we won. On the first evening we were entertained at dinner by the Merion C. C. A large marquee was erected near the Pavilion, and was floored for the occasion. The dinner, which was cooked in Philadelphia, and brought down by train, took place in the marquee. We spent a thoroughly pleasant evening amongst a very jolly and hospitable set of fellows, presided over by the worthy President of the club, Mr. Montgomery. This was the night of the earthquake which did so much damage to Charleston; and whether it was owing to the earthquake or not, certain it is that the "waggon" in which we were being taken to the station after dinner, suddenly came to a stand-still on the road, and as suddenly collapsed, and in a second the merry band of W.I. cricketers were prone in the dust. It *must* have been the earthquake for some of us,—indeed, I shall be more correct if I say *most* of us—fancied we experienced upheavals of mother earth as we afterwards struggled on, on foot, our way to the station. The Merions are very fortunate in their Secretary, Mr. Sayres, one of the pleasantest fellows we met in our tour, and evidently, a most useful and active man in the position he fills. His courtesy and attention to us all were unceasing. Fortunately for us, when we left the Merion club ground, we did not say "good-bye" to the Merions themselves, for many of them kept a watchful eye on us during the whole period of our stay in Philadelphia, and in many ways evinced great good fellowship and extended open handed hospitality to us. Notably, Messrs. Jones, Haites, Rush, Philler, and Law (the popular Captain of the club). And our younger members were especially looked after by Messrs. Barklie, Henry, and Archie Thomson together (afterwards) with Messrs. Brockie, Paterson, Rolston, and others.

Our next match was with the Belmont C. C., whose ground (which is reached by train) is situated a few miles out of Philadelphia. It is a new ground, but has all the makings of a good ground, and doubtless, in a few years it will compare favourably with the other excellent grounds in Philadelphia. The Belmonts have a very handsome Pavilion in which is a room specially fitted up for ladies, with piano, &c., &c.

The Belmont C. C. is peculiar in the large number of lady members belonging to the Club, — about 300. There are 27 Lawn Tennis Courts attached to the Club, and it was a pretty sight on the afternoon on which our Match with the Belmonts was concluded to witness the fair members of the Belmont C. C. crowding into these Courts in which many of them showed excellent play. On the evening of the first day of our Match against the Belmonts we were entertained at supper by them in their handsome pavilion. We found the "Belmonts" a most jovial and pleasant set of fellows, and we all enjoyed our evening with them immensely. Their President, Mr. Green, is a prince among good fellows, and nothing could have been more happy than the manner in which the pleasant evening's doings were presided over by him. He was ably assisted by his namesake (a jovial gentleman who hails from the old country), by Mr. J. A. Scott, the Captain, and Mr. Longstreeth, the Secretary of the Club.

We had a rare musical treat in the Glees which were sung by some members of the Club, who were also members of a well known Glee Club in Philadelphia, and in some solos which were sung by another member of the Club; an excellent comic recitation by Mr. Morgan also dwells pleasantly in our memory. Flitting about from guest to guest during the whole evening, anticipating every want (especially in the item of cigars), and with a bright and cheery smile for everybody was the genial "Sam Knight", a merry fellow, whom we hope we may meet again in the good by-and-by. His attentions in the case of cigars were so marked that our Captain, who never ventures beyond the gentle cigarette, found himself the happy possessor of no less than seven large cigars on his return to his Hotel. A pleasant incident of this evening occurred at its close, when, on our passing through the club room on our way out of the Pavilion, one of the "Belmonts" sat down at the piano, and played "God Save the Queen;" and it is hard to say whether the words of this grand national song were sung more heartily by us who were subjects of our beloved Queen, than by the body of kindly Americans, who had done so much to make the period of our intercourse with them pass sociably and agreeably.

Our next match in Philadelphia was against the Germantown C. C. on their fine ground at Nicetown a few miles out of Philadelphia.

We have memories of a good day's leather-hunting against some excellent batting on the part of some of the Germantown Eleven, and of attention shewn to us by Mr. Welch the President, and Mr. Bissell the Secretary of the Club.

If the Germantown C. C. are fortunate in their Secretary, it is evident that the worthy Secretary is equally fortunate in being the happy possessor of a charming wife, who discoursed pleasantly to us on cricket in particular, and other things in general, and who proved an admirable hostess in her own pleasant home, as at least *one* of our number will cheerfully testify.

Our last match in Philadelphia was against the Young America C. C., which we understood to be one of the oldest Clubs in America.

Here we met some of the veterans of the cricket field of the Continent,— men who have done much to popularize the game in their midst.

The name of Newhall stands out prominently in this connection, and we had the pleasure of seeing two of the brothers (Charlie and Bob) in the Eleven against us. The "Young America" did everything in their power to make our

match with them a pleasant one and in this they fully succeeded, notwithstanding our long spell of leather-hunting. A more pleasant Captain of a team
than E. W. Clarke, it is scarcely possible to meet.

On the whole, we had a capital time in Philadelphia and saw some excellent cricket amongst the several clubs. Whilst in many cases the batting of our
opponents was of a very high order, the fielding, especially of the Belmont's
and Germantown's, could scarcely be surpassed. And I think that the younger
fellows of our party, especially those whose thoughts turn lightly to things of
love, passed many happy hours gazing into the sweet faces, and listening to
the soft voices of the many fair American girls whom they met on the pleasant grounds of the Philadelphia clubs; and I feel sure, to judge from all that
could be seen, that Kerr, Stewart, and Murray Skeete will not readily forget
the two bright girls who so accurately kept the score at the Young America
Match.

Some of us took our leave of Philadelphia on the evening of Wednesday,
the 8th September, and spent that night and the following day in New York;
whilst the rest left Philadelphia early in the afternoon of Thursday, so as to be
in time to catch the steamer leaving New York for "Fall River" en route to
Boston at 5:30 p.m. on the same day. The steamers that run between New
York and Fall River are certainly splendid vessels, traveling at great speed, and
magnificently fitted up. Each carries a fine band of musicians on board; and
[on] our journey from New York we had the good fortune to travel with a
Comedy Opera Company, who very obligingly sang the choicest extracts
from the "Mikado" to the Band accompaniment. Arriving at Fall River at
daybreak on the 10th, we were carried on by train to Boston, a drive of about
one hour and a half.

Our match against the Longwood C. C. at Boston was played on Friday
and Saturday, the 10th and 11th. It was a pleasant and very exciting match, as
the Longwoods, who had only 42 runs to get in their 2nd innings to win the
match, were all put out for 23 runs.

We were most hospitably entertained by the "Longwoods" both on the
cricket ground and at a dinner at the Parker House Hotel on Friday evening.

The cheery president of the club, "Charlie Prince," took the chair, and a
better fellow at the head of a table it is impossible to conceive. The dinner was
excellent; the wines were of the choicest; the hosts were bent on giving us a
good evening, and our own feelings being in unison with their intention, we

enjoyed ourselves thoroughly. We have pleasant recollections of Mr. Lott Mansfield, the hony. secy. of the Longwood C. C., Mr. George Wright, Mr. Hubbard, Mr. McKean and others.

Our last match was against the Staten Island C. C. at Staten Island. This was played on Monday and Tuesday, the 13th and 14th September. Our defeat here was solely owing to the great number of easy catches which were dropped in the most unaccountable manner—very accommodating to our opponents. The Staten Islanders', headed by their pleasant captain, Cyril Wilson, did everything in their power to make the match an enjoyable one; and they gave us a sumptuous dinner at Martinelli's Restaurant in New York on Tuesday evening. The ménu is appended.

Menu.

Huitres sur coquille. Hors d'oeuvres variés. *Sauternes.*

Potage.—Consommé à l'Imperatrice. Poisson. Green Bass à l'Aurora, Pommes Parisiennes.

Rélévé.—Filet de bœuf truffé à la Périgord. *Bordeaux.*

Entrées.—Poulet de Philadelphia à la Portugaise. Rizolle de Ris-do-veau and Epinards. Punch à la Tyrolienne.

Roti.—Philadelphia squabs sur canapé. *Perrier Jouet.*

Salade.—Nix et Mayonnaise.

Dessert.—Satisserie. Glaces, parfait amour, petits fours. Fruit de saison.

Café.—Cognac, Curaçao. Chartreuse.

We met some capital fellows both on the cricket field at Staten Island, and at the dinner above referred to: amongst others Messrs. Cyril Wilson (the Captain already named), Outerbridge (the Secretary of the Club), Emerson Armstrong, George Irvine, Lambkin, Eyre, A. C. Townshend, &c., &c. We had pleasure in making the acquaintance of Mr. Satterthwaite, a leading writer for several American papers on sporting matters, with whom Mr. Wyatt had considerable correspondence before we started on our tour.

On Wednesday, the 15th September, the whole team left New York home-wards. The Jamaican contingent in the Atlas Company's s.s. *Alvo*, the other contingents in Messrs. Leaycraft & Co.'s s.s. *Barracouta*.

A trip thoroughly enjoyable from a cricketing point of view, and rendered still more so from a sociable point of view, by the exceeding kindness and hospitality which was extended to us on all sides, was thus regretfully brought to a close. Let us hope that, as the result of our visit, the bonds of sympathy which always exist between cricketers, no matter whence they hail, may be tightened between ourselves and the cricketers of the great American continent; and that before very many months roll by the familiar faces of some of the many friends whom we met on the cricket grounds of Canada and the United States will be seen on the cricket grounds of our fair isles of the West. When this takes place, I feel sure that the voice of welcome on the part of the West Indian Cricketers will give forth no uncertain sound.

L. F.

Scores and particulars of the Matches played by the West Indian Gentlemen in Canada and the United States—August and September, 1886.

Matches played: 13; 6 won; 5 lost; 2 drawn.

No. 1 Match.

From the Montreal Gazette, 18th August, 1886.

West Indian Gentlemen v. Montreal c. c.—Played at Montreal, 16th & 17th August, 1886.

AN OPEN DRAW.

SCORES.

Montreal.

First Innings.		*Second Innings.*	
Rev. J. A. Newnham, b Lees	0	R. D. Savage, c Fyfe, b Burke	29
F. Stancliffe, c and b Burke	0	A. Taylor, c Fyfe, b Farquharson	4
R. M. Liddell, c L. A. Isaacs, b Farquharson	32	R. M. Liddell, b. Burke	1
Lacey, stpd. Isaacs, b Farquharson	26	Lacey, l b w, b Farquharson	0
P. Barton, B Farquharson	5	F. Stancliffe, c Jenoure, b Stewart	22
E. H. Gough, c Austin, b Burke	20	E. H. Gough, b Stewart	3
J. Smith, c Stewart, b Burke	12	J. Smith, b Stewart	2
A. Taylor, b Burke	6	P. Barton, c L. A. Isaacs, b Stewart	32
W. F. Sills, c Fyfe, b Farquharson	1	W. F. Sills, stpd P. Isaacs, b Stewart	19
A. Fraser, c L. A. Isaacs, b Burke	1	A. Fraser, not out	7
R. D. Savage, not out	0	Rev. J. A. Newnham, b Stewart	1
Extras	9	Extras	10
	112		130

W. I. GENTLEMEN.

First Innings.	Second Innings.
J. Lees, b Lacey 19	J. Lees, c Stancliffe, b Barton 11
L. A. Isaacs, b Lacey 6	E. N. Marshall, B Gough 47
C. J. Annand, l b w, b Savage 7	C. J. Annand, b Lacey 3
W. H. Farquharson, b Lacey 7	L. A. Isaacs, not out 26
L. R. Fyfe, c Lacey, b Gough 3	W. H. Farquharson, c and b Gough 7
R. H. Stewart, c and b Gough 3	L. R. Fyfe, not out 3
E. N. Marshall, not out 9	R. H. Stewart . . . . ⎤
A. F. Austin, c and b Gough 1	Percy Isaacs . . . . ⎟
P. Isaacs, B Gough 0	J. M. Burke . . . . ⎟ To bat
J. M. Burke, b Gough 2	A. F. Austin . . . . ⎟
F. A. Jenoure, c and b Lacey 0	F. A. Jenoure . . . . ⎦
Extras 3	Extras 4
Total 60	Total for 4 wickets 101

BOWLING ANALYSIS.

MONTREAL.

First Innings.	Balls	Mdns.	Rns.	Wkts.	Second Innings.	Balls	Mdns.	Rns.	Wkts.
Burke	70	3	26	5	Burke	96	8	42	2
Lees	124	7	55	1	Farquharson	44	–	21	2
Farquharson	68	5	22	4	Stewart	74	4	34	6
					Marshall	20	1	7	–
					Lees	12	–	6	–
					Isaacs	28	3	10	–

WEST INDIAN GENTLEMEN.

First Innings.	Balls	Mdns.	Rns.	Wkts.	Second Innings.	Balls	Mdns.	Rns.	Wkts.
Sills	32	4	9	0	Gough	68	5	18	2
Savage	24	2	14	1	Lacey	72	2	46	1
Gough	64	7	12	5	Barton	24	0	19	1
Lacey	119	14	22	4	Stancliffe	26	0	14	0

Play in this match was continued under more favourable auspices yesterday, and when the stumps were drawn for the day the result was found to be a very even draw. The wicket in the morning was very heavy from the previous day's rain and runs were difficult to obtain on it during the forenoon, but after lunch it improved greatly and the scoring was much better. During the visitors' first innings the home team fielded extremely well, and the wicket being somewhat difficult during the strangers' innings they were disposed of before luncheon for the small score of 60 runs.

Montreal did better in its second venture, totaling 130, and with 182 runs for the visitors to get in two hours and a half, it was foreseen that the match could not end [in] other than a draw. The West Indians showed capital form, and completely mastering the Montreal bowling, they piled up 101 for the loss of four wickets, when time was called.

TO-DAY'S MATCH.

As previously announced in these columns, the Wanderers from Halifax will meet the West Indians to-day. The majority of the team arrived on Monday night, and the remainder are expected early this morning. From what we know of the Haligonians, it is safe to predict a capital game. They are noted for smart fielding. The whole of the West Indian Team has not yet reached the city, and Messrs. B. T. A. Bell and James Smith, of the Montreal club, will lend their services for the game. Play commences at 10:30 sharp.

No. 2 MATCH.

From the Montreal Gazette, 19th and 20th August.

WEST INDIA GENTLEMEN VS. HALIFAX WANDERERS.—PLAYED AT MONTREAL, ON 18TH & 19TH AUGUST, 1886.

TALL SCORING.

W. I. GENTLEMEN.—*First Innings*

B. T. A. Bell, l b w, b Henry 44	J. M. Burke, c Henry, b Annand 45
J. Lees, c and b Henry 47	A. F. Austin, not out 16
E. N. Marshall, c Henry, b Duffus 38	Extras 19
L. A. Isaacs, b Thompson 12	Total 319
W. H. Farquharson run out. 55	
L. R. Fyfe, c Henry, b Annand 8	
R. H. Stewart, b Kaizer 15	
James Smith, b Thompson 20	
Percy Isaacs, b Kaizer 0	

HALIFAX WANDERERS.

First Innings.

F. A. Kaizer, b Farquharson 14
J. Harris, b Stewart 3
H. Oxley, c L. Isaacs, b Stewart 4
W. A. Henry, b Farquharson 40
C. J. Annand, b. Farquharson 8
W. H. Neal, jr., c Burke, b Farquharson 6
W. S. Duffus, b Burke 16
W. A. Duffus, b Farquharson 2
J. G. Bligh, not out 2
L. J. Fuller, b Burke 0
W. K. Thompson, b Burke 0
Extras 18
Total 113

Second Innings.

W. A. Henry, c P. Isaacs, b Burke 0
F. A. Kaizer, c Burke, b Lees 7
J. Harris, c Lees, b Burke 0
C. J. Annand, stpd. Isaacs, b Lees 5
H. Oxley, b Burke. 10
W. S. Duffus, b Stewart. 12
J. G. Bligh, b Burke 4
W. A. Duffus, b Stewart 8
W. H. Neal, Jr., b Stewart. 2
L. J. Fuller, b Stewart 2
W. K. Thompson, not out 7
Extras 7
Total. 64

BOWLING ANALYSIS.

HALIFAX WANDERERS.

First Innings.

	Overs	Mdns.	Rns.	Wkts.
Burke	38	21	35	3
Stewart	25	9	33	2
Farquharson	21	9	27	5

Second Innings.

	Overs	Mdns.	Rns.	Wkts.
Burke	26	14	20	4
Lees	12	3	23	2
Farquharson	3	2	1	0
Stewart	11	5	13	4

WEST INDIAN GENTLEMEN.

First Innings.

	Balls	Mdns.	Rns.	Wkts.
Thompson	264	24	76	2
Fuller	52	3	32	0
Annand.	188	21	54	2
Kaizer	128	17	55	2
Henry.	88	2	54	2
Duffus	44	–	29	1

The second of the series of interesting contests arranged for the cricket week at Montreal was commenced yesterday. There was a fair attendance. The wicket was still somewhat heavy, but was drying rapidly, and, if anything, the advantage lay with the team fortunate enough to get the use of it. The Haligonian captain won the toss, but, for reasons best known to himself, decided to send his opponents to the wicket, and a few minutes after half-past 10 B. T. A. Bell and J. Lees took up their positions at the crease, the attack being entrusted to Thompson and Fuller, both medium pace over arm bowlers. Thompson led off from the western wicket, and Bell hit his first ball, a full toss hard to the pavilion for 3 and Lees snicked the succeeding one for a single. Lees next hit Fuller twice in succession to the on for a couple, supplemented with a beautiful drive for 4. Oxley was cheered for a very brilliant piece of fielding at long leg. Lees hit Fuller to leg for 3, and scored a couple of singles from the same over, and Bell cut Thompson for 2 and ran a couple of sharp singles off the same bowler. Twenty was soon hoisted, and at 30 Annand took the ball at Fuller's end. This bowler has an awkward high delivery, with a good break from the off. Runs slowed for a little while after this, and both bowlers sent down several maidens. The batsmen were now well set, and at 40 Kaizer went on at the east wicket and Annand changed ends. Kaizer bowled a number of maidens, and the runs, mostly singles, were scored off Annand. Then both batsmen hit the fast round arm bowler to leg for 4; 50, 60, and 70 were telegraphed without any separation, and at 86 Henry went on with slows vice Annand. This bowler's third over resulted in the downfall of Lees, as this batsman in trying a drive was capitally held by Henry. Marshall opened his account with a couple of singles and a brace of nice cuts for a couple. He then drove Henry in fine style for 4. Bell next hit Kaizer twice in succession at the fence for 4, but at 96 an appeal for leg before wicket resulted in his dismissal. Isaacs kept company with Marshall until, at 117 Thompson found an entrance to his stumps with a capital ball. Farquharson and Marshall made another lengthy stand, and bowler after bowler was tried, but still the score mounted up so quickly that 80 runs were added before a brilliant catch by Henry at the on disposed of Marshall for a well earned 38. Fyfe played very patiently for 8, until he, too, fell a victim to another grand catch of Henry—5 for 205. Farquharson continued to score freely, and, aided by some nice contributions from Stewart, the score was still further increased by 28 before the next wicket fell. Farquharson was unfortunately run out when he had earned 55. His long score included five 4's, five 3's, four 2's, and was got by clean hard hitting, combined with good defence. It should be added, however, that he was missed once or twice, but not until he had got well set. James Smith and Burke were also in good form and the huge score was still further augmented by these two batsmen, and for the next half hour some very pretty cricket was witnessed. At 271, however, Smith was clean bowled by Thompson for a nicely earned 20. Austin and Burke, the last men, offered a stubborn resistance and both had some capital hits, notably two grand on drives by Burke and one by Austin, all of which realized 4, and it was not until twenty minutes to five that the last wicket fell for the gigantic total of 319, the greatest number of runs scored on the Montreal ground for a number of years. Burke's innings was conspicuous for its sound defence and vigorous hitting, and his contribution of 45 embraces three 4's, two 3's and six 2's and singles. Austin was left not out with 19 at his credit. Despite their long leather hunting under an almost scorching sun, the Haligonians played a plucky game. Their fielding, although not without blemish, was at times decidedly brilliant. Henry, in the long field and at point, was repeatedly cheered for really grand work, and his catches could not be excelled. Oxley, too, deserves great praise for the distinguished service he rendered his club at long leg. His clean picking up and smart handling of the ball was the subject of much favourable comment. Fuller, Annand and Kaizer, too, are also worthy of special mention in this direction. Their captain displayed excellent judgment in handling his men, and the manner in which he varied the bowling was most judicious. That so many runs were scored against them was to a certain extent due to the state of the wicket, which was most unfavourable to their style of bowling.

With half an hour to spare and in a bad light the Haligonians set to work to reduce, and if possible overtake, the gigantic total against them, and when the stumps were drawn for the day they had lost two wickets for 28 runs. Kaizer and Henry being not out with eleven and two respectively. The Wanderers have some capital batting ability among them, and the result of their doings to-day is anticipated with interest. The match will be resumed at 10.30 (sharp) this forenoon. If the Wanderers can save an inning's defeat, it is all odds that the match, like that of yesterday, will result in a draw. The play to-day will be watched with eager interest.

A GREAT VICTORY.

The West Indies Defeat the Wanderers (Halifax) Early.

Play in this match was resumed a few minutes after 11 o'clock yesterday morning. Kaizer and Henry, the not outs of the previous evening, commenced well. The weather was most favourable, and the wicket, though somewhat cut up with the large amount of run getting on it on the previous day, played much faster and was much favourable to scoring. Overnight the score stood at 28, and through capital play on the sides of both batsmen it was pulled to 59 before a fast ball from Farquharson beat Kaizer. Henry continued to hit freely, and his contribution of 40 was the feature of the Haligonian innings. It included one 4, five 3's, seven 2's, and singles and he received a well merited ovation on his return to the pavilion. W. S. Duffus was the only other player who reached double figures and his innings was characterized by great care and patience. Although he did not come off, W. A. Duffus showed the prettiest style of the lot. His forward play is particularly clean and neat, and altogether this young batsman promises well for the future. The inning terminated shortly after luncheon for 113 runs. The bowling of the West Indians was well on the spot, and the fielding all through the innings was most creditable. With 205 runs to the lead the Haligonians had of course to follow on, and their second venture opened most disastrously for them, the first five men being quickly disposed of for but 26 runs. W. S. Duffus and Oxley, however, made a bit of a stand, and carried the figures to 42 before a separation was effected, Oxley retiring clean bowled after hitting up ten. The two Duffus continued the run getting for some little time longer, but the capital bowling of Stewart and Burke soon asserted itself, and the whole eleven were dismissed in a couple of hours for 64, the West Indians thus gaining a great victory by an innings and 142 runs.

In our report of Wednesday's play it was inadvertently mentioned that Oxley was most prominent in the field at long leg. Neal was the player who distinguished himself in that position. Oxley, however, did some capital work.

The West Indians left the city last evening per C.P.R. for Ottawa, where they will play to-day and to-morrow. A large number of Montreal cricketers assembled at the depot and gave them a most enthusiastic send off. Both teams united in a hearty "Auld Lang Syne" as the train steamed out of the depôt.

From the Toronto Daily Mail, 20th August.

MONTREAL, Aug. 19.—This match was continued this morning at 11 o'clock in perfect cricketing weather, Messrs. Kaiser and Henry, the "not out" men of the previous day, going on with the innings of the Halifax Wanderers to the bowling of Stewart and Burke. Henry opened with 2 threes to leg off Stewart, and scoring became slow, eleven overs being bowled for 8 runs. Oxley was deputed to run for Kaiser, who was hurt by a fast ball from Stewart. The score had reached 50, and Farquharson took the ball from Stewart. Henry hit his second ball to the on for 3, and got Burke to leg for 3 more. At 59 Kaiser was bowled by Farquharson, having put together a very useful 14 by steady batting. Annand joined the Halifax captain, and opened his score with a straight drive for a single. Henry then hit Burke finely to leg for 4, and Annand followed suit with a 4 cut off Farquharson, but succumbed to the next ball from that bowler. Neal went in, but was deprived of Henry's company, who was beaten by a bailer from Farquharson. Henry had played a really excellent and an invaluable innings to 40, giving only half a chance when he had made 25. W. S. Duffus followed, and slipped Farquharson for 4, drove him to the off for 3, and cut Burke for a single. Stewart was tried, vice Burke, and was cut by Neal for 3, but this batsman was easily taken at point at 97. Duffus was joined by his cousin, who after adding two singles fell a victim to Farquharson,—7 for 100.

After luncheon Burke was encharged with the bowling at the west end of the ground. He had bowled excellently all through the innings, but had as yet failed to secure a wicket. He now went to work and performed the great hat trick, dismissing Duffus, Fuller, and Thomson with three successive balls, the innings closing for 113.

Being in a minority of 201 runs the Halifax men had to follow on. Henry and Kaiser went in, and the bowling was given to Burke and Lees. A very disastrous commencement was made. Henry was given out for a catch at the wicket, and Harris was caught in the slips off his first ball. Two for 0. Annand joined Kaiser and drove Lees finely for 3, and Kaiser cut Burke to the pavilion for another 3. Annand was then smartly stumped off Lees. Three for 11. Kaiser gave a hard change to Farquharson at point, and Oxley, the new comer, cut Lees prettily for 3. Kaiser was caught at slip off the next ball, and W. S. Duffus became Oxley's partner, who was bowled by Burke with the total at 26. Bligh went to the bat, and returned the ball hotly to Lees, who failed to hold it. Burke sent down nine overs for 2 runs, and then bowled Bligh with a shooter, and a moment after Stewart bowled Duffus with a slow ball. A few runs were added, and Fuller was dismissed by the last named bowler. Nine for 52. Thompson got 2 to the on and 3 to leg off. Stewart was missed at point by Farquharson, and put Burke through the slips for 2. Duffus was then bowled by Stewart, the total being 64, or a victory for the West Indies by an innings and and 142 runs. In the first innings Burke took

3 wickets for 35, Stewart 2 for 33, Farquharson 5 for 27. In the second innings Burke took 4 wickets for 19, Lees took 2 wickets for 13, Stewart took 4 wickets for 13.

<hr>

No. 3 Match.

From Ottawa Daily Citizen, 23rd August.

<hr>

West Indians v. Ottawa c. c.

<hr>

W. I. Gentlemen.

First Innings.		*Second Innings.*	
J. Lees, b Coste	o	J. Lees, b Steele	o
E. M. Skeete, run out	15	E. M. Skeete, c Austin, b Steele	21
G. Wyatt, b Steele	1	R. H. Stewart, s Powell, c Steele	4
W. H. Farquharson, c Powell, b Coste	11	J. M. Burke, run out	15
L. Isaacs, b Coste	o	W. H. Farquharson. b Steele	o
R. H. Stewat, b Steele	8	G. Wyatt, l b w, b Coste	28
T. Skeete, run out	6	T. Skeete, b Steele	o
W. Collymore, c Powell, b Steele	4	L. Fyfe, b F. H. Smith	o
L. Fyfe, c Powell, b Steele	o	L. Isaacs, c Steele, b F. H. Smith	o
J. M. Burke, not out	5	A. Swain, not out	4
A. Swain, c A. G. Smith, b Coste	6	W. Collymore, b Steele	3
Extras	11	Extras	5
Total	67	Total	80

Ottawa.

First Innings.		*Second Innings.*	
V. H. Steele, c and b Lees	15	V. H. Steele, c Farquharson, b Burke	20
A. F. Austin, b Stewart	o	J. E. Smith, b Burke	7
L. Coste, b Stewart	4	A. G. Smith, b Burke	4
A. G. Smith, s Wyatt, b Lees	22	L. Coste, b Farquharson	1
F. H. Smith, run out	1	F. H. Smith, not out	9
E. G. Powell, run out	4	C. L. Lawrence, b Farquharson	5
W. Makinson, b Burke	o	E. G. Powell, run out	o
C. L. Lawrence, c Farquharson, b Burke	1	A. F. Austin, b Farquharson	3
E. J. Smith, not out	9	F. W. Hamilton, b Farquharson	o
F. W. Hamilton, b Lees	2	T. B. Taylor, b Farquharson	1
P. B. Taylor, b Burke	4	W. Makinson, b Farquharson	o
Extras	5	Extras	4
Total	67	Total	54

BOWLING ANALYSIS.

W. I. GENTLEMEN.

First Innings.	Balls	Mdns.	Rns.	Wkts.		*Second Innings.*	Balls	Mdns.	Rns.	Wkts.
Coste	127	20	21	4		Coste	124	16	28	1
Smith	16	1	4	0		Steele	128	9	47	6
Steele	112	12	31	4		Smith	4	1	–	2

Mr. Smith bowled 4 wides in the two innings.

OTTAWA.

First Innings.	Balls	Mdns.	Rns.	Wkts.		*Second Innings.*	Balls	Mdns.	Rns.	Wkts.
Burke	87	8	22	3		Burke	96	10	28	3
Stewart	24	–	17	2		Farquharson	76	10	19	6
Farquharson	4	–	6	–		Stewart	26	3	3	–
Lees	40	3	13	3						
Skeete	16	1	4	–						

Mr. Skeete bowled 1 wide in the first innings.

———

The match between the West India cricketers and the Ottawa eleven was resumed at Rideau Hall, Saturday morning, Mr. G. Wyatt, not out 28, and Mr. Swain facing the bowling of Steele and Coste. The former was immediately disposed of and Mr. Collymore joined Mr. Swain. These two added 7 runs to the score, and the second innings was brought to a close for 80 runs. After a brief interval, the Ottawas entered upon their second essay with 81 runs to make to win, but contrary to general expectation, only scored 54, and therefore lost the match by 26 runs. The second innings of the Ottawa opened with Messrs. V. H. Steele and E. J. Smith at the bat, facing the deliveries of Messrs. Burke and Farquharson. Runs came slowly at first, both batsmen displaying sound defence. With the score at 17 Mr. E. J. Smith was clean bowled by a bailer from Burke. Mr. A. G. Smith filled the vacancy, but only added 4 to the score, when Burke upset his bails by a similar ball. Mr. Coste was next on the list, but his stay was of short duration, a magnificent leg break being too much for him. Mr. F. H. Smith came next to assist Mr. Steele who was playing grand cricket, and it looked as if these two careful players would give considerable trouble, but with a few runs added, Mr. Farquharson caught Steele off Burke in the slips. His innings of 20 was made by careful play and included several fine leg hits. After the departure of Steele none of the others made any stand, and Mr. F. H. Smith carried out his bat for 9 well-earned runs, having seen the fall of 7 wickets during his innings. For the winners Messrs. Burke and Farquharson bowled remarkably well, and were well supported in the field.

———

From the Montreal Gazette, 21st August.

OTTAWA, August 20th.—In the cricket match between the West Indian and Ottawa Cricket club teams, played here to-day, the visitors went first to the bat and were all disposed of for 67 runs. The bowling of Coste and Steele, of Ottawa, was excellent. The Ottawas in their first innings made 67 also, creating a tie. In their second innings the West India team scored 73 for the loss of eight wickets, when play was stopped for the day.

OTTAWA, August 21.—The second innings of the match between the West India gentlemen cricketers and a team of the Ottawa club was concluded this afternoon, the West Indians scoring 80 to 54 of the Ottawa and winning the match by 26 runs, the first inning having resulted in a tie. The visiting team left for Toronto at 11.30 this evening.

———

No. 4 Match.

From Toronto Daily Globe, 25th August.

West Indian Gentlemen v. Toronto.

West Indian gentlemen.—*First Innings.*

J. Lees (Jamaica), c Saunders, b Jones 31	L. Fyfe (Jamaica), b Boyd 1
E. M. Skeete (B'dos), b Boyd 32	A. W. Swain (Demerara), c Saunders,
G. Wyatt (Demerara), b Jones 4	b Boyd 2
L. Kerr (Demerara), b Boyd 2	J. M. Burke (Jam.), b Saunders 11
W. H. Farquharson (Jamaica), run out 38	P. Isaacs (Jam.), l b w, b Marsh 10
E. N. Marshall (Jam.), b Boyd 16	W. O. Collymore (B'dos), not out 0
R. H. Stewart (Demerara), c Saunders,	Extras 13
b Lindsay 7	167

Toronto. c. c.

First Innings.	*Second Innings.*
W. W. Vickers, c Skeete, b Burke 0	W. W. Vickers, c Burke, b Stewart. 10
W. D. Saunders, b Burke 11	W. D. Saunders, c Collymore, b Burke. 0
A. W. Winslow, b Burke 6	A. W. Winslow, c Stewart, b Burke. 0
G. W. Marsh, b Burke. 3	G. W. Marsh, c Burke, b Farquharson 12
W. W. Jones, run out 22	W. W. Jones, c Farquharson, b Burke 0
M. Boyd, c Fyfe, b Farquharson 8	M. Boyd, c Wyatt, b Burke. 0
W. F. W. Creelman, b Burke 1	W. F. W. Creelman, b Burke. 4
F. S. Dickey, c Isaacs, b Farquharson. 7	F. S. Dickey, not out 13
G. G. S. Lindsay, b Burke 3	G. G. S. Lindsay, c Lees, b Farquharson 0
G. B. Behan, c & b Farquharson 0	G. B. Behan, c Stewart, b Farquharson 13
A. G. Brown, c Wyatt, b Farquharson. 3	A. G. Brown, c Fyfe, b Stewart 3
A. Collins, not out 0	A. Collins, b Burke. 0
Extras. 7	Extras. 2
71	57

BOWLING ANALYSIS.

Toronto.

First Innings.	Ovs.	Mdns.	Rns.	Wkts.	*Second Innings.*	Ovs.	Mdns.	Rns.	Wkts.
Burke.	24	10	31	6	Burke.	19.3	13	10	6
Farquharson	23.1	9	33	4	Farquharson	27	14	30	3
					Stewart	12	8	9	2
					Swain	5	2	6	0

WEST INDIANS.

	Overs	Mdns.	Rns.	Wkts.
Marsh 22.2		13	24	1
Boyd 49		27	37	5
Jones 31		6	57	2
Lindsay 16		8	14	1
Behan 9		2	17	0
Saunders 4		1	5	1

Marsh bowled two wides and Jones one; Boyd bowled a no-ball.

———

Cricketers are proverbially lucky in the choice of their days for matches, but the drizzling rain throughout yesterday rather contradicted this belief. The wicket suffered severely, and at no time played up to its usual celerity. Scoring was slow, and the batting of the West Indians was the most patient and least lively of any which has been seen on the ground this year. The Toronto fielding was not good, and the bowling of Boyd alone is worthy of comment. His analysis shows 5 wickets for 37 runs. The toss was won by the visitors, and they took the innings. Lees and Skeete were opposed by Marsh and Boyd, and for many overs the bowlers kept the batsmen on the defence. Finally a leg-bye was run, and the game opened in real earnest. The runs, however, were a very long time coming, and the few spectators who had gathered to see the commencement of the match were rather disappointed in this lack of brilliancy on the part of the West Indians. As the result proved, the pair which stood the brunt of the attack, resisting all temptations to hit half volleys, and playing the good balls with a straight bat, were determined to remain there, if steadiness combined with art would do the trick. Lee's batting was much more finished than that of his companion, but the colt had got 32 when Boyd found his wicket. At that juncture 67 was signalled for the loss of one wicket. The fall of another wicket two runs later brightened up the fielders considerably, and a more hopeful outlook appeared. Farquharson, the giant of the team, came to the front a little later, and he showed considerable fight. He hit Jones around the field, especially to the leg. He was missed in the long field on, but the chance was a difficult one. A variety of bowling had been tried, and the wickets were still falling very slowly. When luncheon was announced five wickets were down for 98 runs. After the marquee had been visited a start was made again. Farquharson again showed some brilliant hitting, chiefly to leg, and the score crept up into three figures. Burke seconded Farquharson's effort in a very encouraging style, and between them the score was brought to 154, when Burke succumbed to a good one from Saunders, who had doffed his pads and gloves for the occasion. P. Isaacs came next, but Farquharson ran himself out, having obtained the handsome total of 38 by his strong and safe play. Three more runs were added to the score, and then Isaac was retired on a leg before decision. The innings total was 167, of which number 13 were extras, 3 only of which were out-and-out byes. The innings lasted from 11.30 until 4.30. The first wicket was a hard one to get, and the bowling became demoralized before the stubborn defence. The Toronto men were even more unfortunate as regards the weather than their opponents, since the rain now fell faster than at any time in the day. The light was bad too, and it is in a great measure accountable for the excellence of the bowling record of Burke. W. W. Jones played freely and well and seemed well set with 16 to credit when time was called for the night. Creelman and he ran some very short runs which seemed to tickle the spectators immensely. Six wickets have fallen for 55 runs, and before the eleventh wicket falls 32 runs must be got to save a follow-on. The result depends greatly on to-day's weather, but in any case the match ought to be interesting and worthy of a thought on the part of the cricketers in the city.

There are two spare men with the team, L. A. Isaacs and T. Skeete, and a spectator in the person of the veteran Mr. C. Isaacs.

SECOND DAY'S PLAY.

The match came to an untimely end yesterday at the early hour of 2 o'clock. The weather did not mend much, and was again disagreeable. The wicket was poor and bumpy, in addition being sticky. Jones and Dickey, the not-outs of the previous day, resumed their places at the wickets at 11 o'clock, and Jones led off capitally. He got five more runs, 22 in all, and, then calling on his partner for a short run, to which there was no response, he was run out before he could scramble back. It was a pity, as thirty more runs were required to save a follow-on. None of the remaining batsmen did anything worthy of note, and at 11.40 all were out for 71, some 96 runs behind their opponents. The follow-on was thus inevitable, and Captain Saunders sent in Jones and Lindsay to act on the offensive. The task was by no means an impossible one, but on that wicket extremely difficult of accomplishment. The opening wickets fell in one, two, three order, not a run being signalled to the scoring stand. Vickers relieved the monotony by putting Burke to leg for a single. Collins then retired, clean bowled by Burke. Four wickets for one run. Saunders joined Vickers who got four more runs, and then the Captain skied one over the bowler's head, which was well taken by Collymore. Six wickets for five runs was even more disastrous; but a change, though a slight one, appeared. Marsh and Vickers helped the total to 23, when Vickers fell with 10 runs to his credit. Marsh did not long survive, but his dozen was a very acceptable contribution. It was reserved to Dickey and Behan to do something towards the demoralization of the foreign bowling. Between them the score was raised from 27 to 50, each batsman scoring 15 runs. Behan hit in strong form, while Dickey, playing more cautiously, depended on cuts and snicks for his runs. The innings and match ended at 2.15. The West Indians beat the home team by an innings and 39 runs. Burke's analysis in the second innings was excellent. Everyone was glad to see the West Indians win, but their majority was larger than any one anticipated. A match will be begun this morning, at 10.30, between the same team and an eleven chosen from the Ontario Association. L. Kerr was unable, on account of sickness, to play yesterday, and a substitute was found for him.

No. 5 MATCH.

From the Toronto Mail, 26th & 27th August.

WEST INDIAN GENTLEMEN V. ONTARIO ASSOCIATION.

WEST INDIAN GENTLEMEN.

First Innings.	Second Innings.
J. Lees, c Coste, b Smith 13	J. Lees, l b w, b Smith 34
E. M. Skeete, b Smith 7	E. M. Skeete, b A. C. Allan 3
P. A. Isaacs, run out 2	R. H. Stewart, c Lloyd-Jones, b Coste 4
W. H. Farquharson, c Saunders, b Smith 1	E. N. Marshall, b Coste 25
G. Wyatt, c Vickers, b Smith 0	W. H. Farquharson, b A. C. Allan 19
R. H. Stewart, c Smith b Coste 15	G. Wyatt, st. Saunders, b Coste 0
E. N. Marshall, b A. C. Allan 4	T. Skeete, b A. C. Allan 10
J. M. Burke, c Lloyd Jones, b Smith 0	L. A. Isaacs, b A. C. Allen 0
L. L. Kerr, b Smith 4	P. A. Isaacs, c Marsh, b A. C. Allan 1
L. R. Fyfe, c Winslow, b Smith 1	L. Kerr, c Saunders, b A. C. Allan 4
T. S. Skeete, not out 0	J. M. Burke, not out 1
L. Isaacs, b Smith 0	L. Fyfe, b A. C. Allan 0
Extras 4	Extras 8
Total 51	Total 109

ONTARIO ASSOCIATION.

First Innings.

W. W. Vickers (Toronto),
  c Farquharson, b Marshall 32
D. W. Saunders (Toronto),
  c Marshall, b Burke 9
W. W. Jones (Toronto), c L. Isaacs, b Burke . . 0
F. G. A. Allan (Trinity School), b Stewart . . 22
T. Biggs (Orillia), c Marshall, b Burke 5
S. D. Smith (Gooderham & Worts),
  s P. Isaacs, b Stewart 18
A. C. Allan (Toronto), b Stewart 0
A. Winslow (Toronto), b Lees 1
A. Lloyd-Jones (Simcoe), b Stewart 1
L. Coste (Amherstburg), c Marshall, b Lees . . 3
H. J. Bethune (Toronto), c P. Isaacs, b Lees . . 5
G. W. Marsh (Toronto), not out 0
Extras 5
Total 101

Second Innings.

W. W. Vickers, b Burke 7
D. W. Saunders, c Stewart,
  b Farquharson 12
W. W. Jones, c Kerr, b Farquharson 0
F. G. B. Allan, c Kerr, b Burke 0
J. Biggs, b Burke 7
A. C. Allan, c P. Isaacs, b Farquharson 2
G. W. Marsh, b Burke 0
A.T. Winslow, c Fyfe, b Farquharson 7
S. D. Smith, c Wyatt, b Burke 6
L. Coste, c Burke, b Farquharson 0
A. Lloyd-Jones, c P. Isaacs,
  b Farquharson 0
H. J. Bethune, not out 0
Extras 2
Total 43

BOWLING ANALYSIS.

WEST INDIAN GENTLEMEN.

First Innings.	Overs	Mdns.	Rns.	Wkts.
Smith	31	14	28	8
Coste	17	12	8	1
Jones	6	3	5	0
A. C. Allan	8	6	6	1

Second Innings.	Overs	Mdns.	Rns.	Wkts.
Smith	48	37	41	1
Coste	33	13	43	3
Allan, A.C	19	16	4	7
Marsh	5	4	3	0
Lloyd-Jones	5	2	10	0

ONTARIO ASSOCIATION.

First Innings.	Overs	Mdns.	Rns.	Wkts.
Burke	23	10	28	3
Farquharson	13	3	29	0
Stewart	15	5	16	4
Marshall	4	2	7	1
Lees	10	3	16	3

Second Innings.	Overs	Mdns.	Rns.	Wkts.
Burke	26	15	20	5
Farquharson	26	15	21	6

There was a much larger attendance of spectators at the Toronto cricket grounds yesterday than on the previous days, the weather at last permitting admirers of cricket to gratify their taste by witnessing the play of the visitors from the West Indies. Private carriages lined the side of the grounds overlooking the lawn, the large branches of the trees forming a most acceptable shelter from the uncomfortably warm rays of the sun.

The visitors were first to handle the willow, and those who had witnessed their batting in the match with the Toronto Cricket Club were surprised to see how rapidly the wickets fell. J. Lees and E. M. Skeete, who had made such a grand stand when opening the match on Monday, were disposed of for a total between them of 20. Of this number Lees contributed 13, acquired by patient, steady play. The top scorer of the innings was R. H. Stewart, who put together 15 in good style. No one else reached double figures, and when the last wicket fell, the telegraph announced a total of 51. The fielding of the Ontario players was sharp and clean.

The home team sent in Vickers and Saunders to defend the wickets. A most encouraging commencement was made. Vickers piled up runs very rapidly, two leg hits contributing 5 each. When he was caught out by Farquharson the board credited him with the fine total of 32. F. G. B. Allan, by good steady batting, put together 22. This total consisted of 9 twos and 4 singles. The only other man to get into double figures was S. B. Smith. In his total of 18 there was one six. The hit was really not good for more than 3, but a hunt for a lost ball allowed three more to be trotted out. Saunders was unfortunate, but in his total of 9 there were two threes. When A. C. Allan came to the bat he was clean bowled by Stewart with the first, a full-pitched ball. The innings closed for 101. The West Indians were not fielding in as good form as on Monday, and several chances were missed.

The Ontario eleven now seemed to have a clear path to victory, but the way the West Indians began batting in their second innings created fresh doubt as to the result. Lees and Skeete were the first to face the bowlers, Skeete was disposed of for 3, and Stewart who succeeded him, for 4. Then Marshall came on, and from now until time was called the runs were made rapidly. When six o'clock arrived, 57 runs had been obtained for the loss of two wickets. The bowling of Burke and Stewart called forth many expressions of commendation, and as the analysis will show, Smith was also very effective.

There was a most exciting finish to the match, yesterday, between the West Indies team and Ontario Association. There was a good attendance of spectators, the fine weather and expectation of a close match inducing a large turn out. When time was called on Wednesday evening each team had completed one innings. Two wickets had gone down, and the not outs were Messrs. J. Lees and E. N. Marshall. Mr. Lees had already run up 30, and Mr. Marshall, with 14, was evincing an inclination to follow his example in reaching high figures, Messrs. Skeete and Stewart having contributed 3, and 4, respectively, and six extras added made the total 57 when play ceased for the day.

The second innings of the West Indians was resumed yesterday morning, and the bowlers were not long at work when Lees was declared out leg before wicket. He was loudly applauded as he made his way to the pavilion, and certainly deserved this recognition of his superior batting. His total of 34 was made without a change, and his defence of the wicket should have been of longer duration. Ontario's umpire was in error when he gave him out leg before wicket, and the mistake was freely acknowledged by members of the home team. Marshall added 9 to his previous day's score, and retired with 25 runs to his credit. The board registered 109 when the last wicket fell. The bowling of A. C. Allan was remarkably fine, and the fielding of the Ontario men was good throughout.

The home team began the second innings with 60 runs to win. It seemed a comparatively easy task, and everybody supposed that the West Indies were going to meet with their first defeat. Probably the visitors held the same opinion, but they went out to do their best, and in more than one sense could not have done better. Vickers and Saunders went in to face the bowling of Burke and Farquharson. For a little while the runs ran up merrily, but presently Vickers was clean bowled by Burke for 7, and was soon followed by Saunders, who was prettily caught out after getting 12 runs together. Jones and F. G. Allan each put a cipher opposite his name in the score book, and there were 4 wickets gone for 19 runs. The wickets now fell rapidly, the only pair to make any kind of a stand being formed of Winslow and Smith. When the eight wicket had gone the telegraph announced 43. This total was not increased, the following three batsmen being unable to add to the score. The fielding of the West Indians during this innings was especially close and sharp, and the bowling of Burke and Farquharson, who remained in office till the last wicket went down, even surpassed their previous work of the week. Mr. P. Isaacs proved himself to be an excellent wicket-keeper.

From the Globe, 27th August, 1886.

Captain Fyfe seems to be a lucky man in winning the toss twice in succession, and on each occasion his team enjoyed the best of the wicket. Captain Saunders marshaled his team in the field at 11.10, and entrusted the bowling to S. D. Smith and D. L. Coste. E. M. Skeete and Lees were the first batsmen to appear, and the fielders having seen these men bat on the previous day prepared to do their utmost to effect their riddance. Thirty-five minutes passed, and the batsmen's wickets were still intact, but the score had only risen to 15. Skeete was cleverly bowled by Smith with the telegraph still showing that number. Three more wickets fell in short order, including Lees, who was neatly snapped up by Coste at draw-leg off Smith. Lees played in very good style, and his stubborn defence was worth witnessing. His score was 13. Stewart saved the innings from total demoralization by running up 15 just in the nick of time. He played prettily and well for his addition to the score. The innings closed a minute or two after one o'clock for the meager total of 51. The fielding of the Ontario men was excellent, and Smith's bowling phenomenal. Luncheon was disposed of, and at 2.10 Vickers and Saunders took up their positions at the wickets. Burke held the leather at the northern end and delivered to Vickers. Then began some rapid scoring on the part of the batsmen, Vickers jumping into both Burke and Farquharson. The bulletin board showed the doubles in rapid succession until 40 was reached, and a few runs later Saunder's wicket fell for a carefully made 9. Vickers was taken in the next over by Farquharson at point off Marshall for 32. This contribution was made up of 2 fives, 2 threes, 3 twos, and singles. Two wickets for 44. Jones failed to score. F. G. B. Allan, Trinity College School, now came in, and his advent was watched with great interest, since it was his first match of importance. His play was strong, and his selection reflected great credit on the Association Committee. Between him and Smith the runs came in apace, and before the latter was dismissed the total had been raised to 84. Smith played capitally for his 18. Allan's performance in getting 22 runs was very meritorious, and his cricketing career will be doubtless fraught with much success in the future. The side was all out for 101, or fifty runs more than the West Indians were able to get. The West Indian fielding has deteriorated somewhat, a number of easy flies being missed in the field. The bowling too was rather demoralized early in the innings, but later it picked up very much under the more favourable circumstances. The second venture of the West Indians was of a different character to the first. Despite the best efforts of Smith, Coste, and Allan, the first pair of batsmen could not be dislodged until 25 runs were put on. E. M. Skeete was the unfortunate one, having kept up his wickets 40 minutes for 3 runs. Stewart fell at 30, but at six o'clock Lees was still on the defensive with 30 runs to his credit, and Marshall rapidly closing upon him with nearly half that number. Lees played with great care, and gave no chances, his back play being stronger than at any time previous.

———

From the World, 27th August, 1886.

Once more the West Indians have trounced a Canadian team. The match was a very interesting one, and when the Ontario representatives had only 60 runs to win, it was looked upon as [as] good as won. Marvellous to relate the provincial team only got 43, and were thus beaten by 17 runs, after a most exciting finish. The features of the innings were the capital fielding and bowling of the West Indians, who did up the home men to a turn.

———

No. 6 Match.

From the Hamilton Evening Times, 28th and 30th August.

———

West Indians v. Hamilton c. c.

———

West Indians.

First Innings.		*Second Innings.*	
J. Lees, c Patterson, b Gillespie	2	J. Lees, b Gillespie	6
E. M. Skeete, run out	23	E. M. Skeete, c Kennedy, b Gillespie	3
T. S. Skeete, b Ferrie	1	T. S. Skeete, not out	8
E. N. Marshall, b Gillespie	10	E. N. Marshall, run out	10
W. H. Farquharson, c Patterson, b Ferrie	10	W. H. Farquharson, b Ferrie	3
R. H. Stewart, run out	4	R. H. Stewart, b Cummings	2
L. L. Kerr, c Patterson, b Gillespie	11	L. L. Kerr, c and b Ferrie	1
L. R. Fyfe, b Cummings	4	L. R. Fyfe, b Ferrie	3
W. Collymore, c Patterson, b Ferrie	1	W. Collymore, b Ferrie	2
P. Isaacs, not out	12	P. Isaacs, l b w, b Kennedy	21
A. Swain, c Robertson, b Gillespie	27	A. Swain, c A. Patterson, b Kennedy	0
Extras	9	Extras	4
Total	114	Total	63

HAMILTON.

First Innings.	
Woolverton, c Marshall, b Farquharson	5
Patterson, c Farquharson, b Stewart	2
Gillespie, b Farquharson	8
Francis, c Isaacs, b Farquharson	6
Guthrie, run out	0
Cummings, b Farquharson	15
Dixon, b Lees	21
Ferrie, b Farquharson	14
Robertson, c Collymore, b Lees	11
Harvey, b Lees	16
Kennedy, not out	0
Extras	18
Total	116

Second Innings.	
Gillespie, c Marshall, b Stewart	2
Francis, not out	11
Guthrie, b Stewart	20
Cummings, not out	8
Harvey, c Kerr, b Farquharson	15
Woolverton	
Patterson	
Dixon	Did not bat
Ferrie	
Robertson	
Kennedy	
Extras	7
Total	63

BOWLING ANALYSIS.

HAMILTON

First Innings.	Overs	Mdns.	Rns.	Wkts.
Farquharson	29	13	38	5
Stewart	16	5	28	1
Swain	3	1	8	0
Marshall	14	6	10	0
Lees	11	4	14	3

Second Innings.	Overs	Mdns.	Rns.	Wkts.
Stewart	10	1	27	2
Farquharson	11	3	26	1
Lees	2	0	3	0

WEST INDIANS.

First Innings.	Overs	Mdns.	Rns.	Wkts.
Ferrie	46	24	46	3
Gillespie	39	22	30	4
Francis	4	3	7	0
Cummings	9	3	18	1
Kennedy	3	2	4	0

Second Innings.	Overs	Mdns.	Rns.	Wkts.
Ferrie	22.2	8	25	4
Gillespie	23	13	15	2
Cummings	8	1	10	1
Kennedy	7	3	9	2

THE HAMILTON TEAM GETS AHEAD OF THE WEST INDIANS ON THE FIRST INNINGS.

The weather yesterday afternoon was bright and pleasant enough for those who sat in the shade and watched the West Indian and Hamilton teams play cricket, but it was red hot work for those who took part in the game. One of the visitors, whose home is in Jamaica, said that yesterday would have been considered a very hot day on that island, where the heat of the sun is tempered by the sea breeze. The weather, however, did not prevent the teams from playing good cricket, and the large number of spectators who assembled during the afternoon had a thoroughly enjoyable time, The "Times'" report yesterday closed at lunch time. After that necessary and rather pleasant break in the proceedings, play was resumed, Kerr and Collymore at bat for the visitors. The latter retired after getting one, being neatly caught by Patterson. Cummings bowled a couple of overs, and then Gillespie went on. They changed back again shortly, but Swain and Isaacs were well set. Swain did not seem to have much difficulty with the bowling, and batted out 2 four's and a three off Cummings, followed by a three off Captain Kennedy's bowling, for he also tried his hand on the batsman that was making the best stand of the day. Swain continued to score and Gillespie took the ball again. The telegraph showed the century off his first ball, but Swain was finally caught by Robertson on a nice high ball, and the visitors' last wicket fell at 4 o'clock for 114. The innings was well played and the fielding of the home team was good. Few chances were missed and few bad throws were made. The good score of the visitors against the bowling that won the International match for Canada shows fine batting ability.

Hamilton's first innings began at 4.30, Woolverton and Patterson batting the bowling of Farquharson and Stewart. Patterson was quickly retired, as he unfortunately gave Farquharson an easy chance which the latter accepted. Gillespie joined the doctor, and they had 20 up when the former was bowled by Farquharson. He had batted strong when he was in, and there was much disappointment when he retired so quickly. Francis took his place, but had not the governor's company long, as Woolverton was caught by Marshall. Guthrie and Francis then faced the bowlers, and in too great eagerness to make a run Guthrie was stumped. Four wickets for 25. Cummings took his place and soon was well set and batting hard. He speedily got into double figures. The fielding of the visitors was sharp, but the expectations of the spectators for a longer stand were disappointed. Cummings was bowled for 15. Five wickets for 45. Ferrie and Francis joined partnership. When they had been in a short time the visitors made a change in the bowling, and Swain went on at Stewart's end. Francis was soon caught at the wicket. The half-century then went up on the telegraph and Ferrie continued batting for 3's and 2's till a further change in the bowling was made, Swain being relieved by Marshall. The Hamilton men still kept hitting, and had 22 between them when stumps were drawn at 6 o'clock. Hamilton had then 70 runs and six wickets down.

This morning play was resumed at 11.20 on a first-class wicket and under a blazing sun. Dixon and Ferrie, the not-outs of last night, went to the bat. Hamilton made a bad beginning, Farquharson's second ball taking Ferrie's wickets. Harvey succeeded him and began scoring fast. Dixon, who partnered him, batted carefully and well, and Lee's bowling was tried in place of Farquharson's, and the batters seemed to like it; but after Dixon had made half a dozen off it, Lees bowled him, and he retired with a well-earned score of 21, amid the plaudits of the spectators. Robertson was caught out by Collymore at 113 runs, lacking one of a tie. Kennedy and Harvey were then sent in, and Harvey raised the Hamilton score to 116. Harvey was bowled by Lees in a few minutes after being joined by Kennedy, and the innings closed for 116.

The game will probably be a draw, as both sides can hardly finish a second innings.

Entertained.

The visitors were entertained at dinner at the Hamilton Club last evening, Mr. R. E. Kennedy, captain of the home tea, occupying the chair. The toast of "Our Guests" was responded to by Mr. L. R. Fyfe and Mr. Guy Wyatt, who expressed themselves as delighted with their reception and with all they had seen in this city. They had heard of Hamilton and her hospitality, but what they had experienced had exceeded their anticipations. Songs were contributed by Messrs. Farquharson and Lees, of Jamaica, Stinson and MacKelchan, of this city, and a very pleasant evening was spent, the company breaking up about 11.30.

———

The Hamilton Team Victorious.

The visitors began their second innings at 12.30 on Saturday, Gillespie and Ferrie bowling from the north and south ends respectively. Lees and E. M. Skeete were the first to bat.

The bowling was strong and well on the wicket, and only 3 had been got when Skeete, who had the top score on Friday, was caught out by Kennedy. Lees and Isaacs played carefully, but slowly, and the total was but 14 when the gallant lieutenant's stumps were taken. When the telegraph showed 20, Cummings went on to bowl with Gillespie. Cummings soon began work by taking Stewart's stumps on a "yorker." Three wickets for 23 runs. Farquharson and Isaacs were now at bat, and much was expected of them. But few runs were made before Ferrie and Cummings changed again, and with his second ball Ferrie sent Farquharson's middle wicket flying and the big batter retired, having only 3 to his credit. Isaacs had been playing a steady, but free hitting game. Runs came very slowly while he and Marshall were in together, but the batsmen played a cautious game, and continued to score off both bowlers. Kennedy took Gillespie's place at the wickets, and the change proved a profitable one, as after an over or two he sent a puzzler down to Isaacs, which the latter attempted to bat by stepping in front of the wickets. He succeeded in blocking the ball, but with his nether extremities, and was given out. His score of one 4, one 3, three 2's and singles was earned by good all-round cricket. With the score at 47 for five wickets down, an adjournment was made for lunch. On resuming, Swain, who made the top score of 27 on Friday, joined Marshall, but was very soon retired by a smart catch at long-on by F. Patterson, who had taken Woolverton's place for a short time. This cheering result, from the home team's point of view, was secured in a maiden over by Kennedy, who had two wickets within the same over. Fyfe, the veteran captain, joined Marshall, and began by hitting Kennedy hard towards the grand stand. Two runs were scored and an attempt was made to steal a third, when Patterson, who fielded the ball, sent it in with lightning speed to his brother the wicket-keeper, who scattered the stumps before the arrival of Marshall. This left the score at 47. Ferrie immediately after sent the ball right into the centre stump of Fyfe's wicket, and it began to be evident that the visitors stood little chance of gaining a victory. Through a brilliant one-hand catch by Ferrie, Kerr, the ninth man, was compelled to retire, while the score had only been added to by 1. Nine wickets for 53 runs. Skeete and Collymore, the two last men, continued to play a careful game and runs came slowly. Gillespie did some fine bowling, six successive maidens being registered to his credit. He had thirteen maidens out of his twenty-three overs. The partnership of batsmen existed for nearly an hour, and it looked as if another change in the bowling would have to be resorted to, when Ferrie clean bowled Collymore, and the innings ended at 3.20, Collymore having to be contented with 2, while T. S. Skeete, the not out, had 8.

The innings closing for 63, left the Hamilton eleven 62 to win, and the home team went to bat at 3.40 with the assurance that a comparatively easy victory would be theirs. Guthrie and Harvey were sent to the bat, and the bowlers were Stewart and Farquharson. Both batters opened out in excellent form, and gave a magnificent exhibition of all-round hitting. Guthrie finally knocked a ball from Stewart into his wicket, and was compelled to retire after a brilliant innings of 20. In a comparatively short time he had put together one 6, obtained by a hit away over the eastern fence—by far the biggest hit made on the Hamilton grounds this season—two 4's, two 2's and singles. He was heartily congratulated on his retirement. One wicket for 36. Gillespie now joined Harvey, and the run getting continued, the latter, Harvey, playing a careful game till he was caught by Kerr behind the wickets. Kerr had taken the place of Isaacs, who had been compelled to retire on account of a finger being put out of joint. Harvey's 15 were obtained by the best of cricket His score was made up of one 4, four 2's, and singles. For such a record by so young a cricketer, and against the best bowlers that the West Indians could produce, it was most creditable. Two wickets for 42. Gillespie failed to bat up to his record, being caught out by Marshall at long-on off a ball from Stewart. Three wickets for 42. Francis who had taken his place, was joined by Cummings, the "slugging" hitter of the Hamilton team, and both batsmen went at it with a will, getting on to the bowling of both trundlers from the start. It is hard to say how many runs they might have contributed to the score—so rapidly was it being added to by singles, doubles and triplets—if it had been necessary to prolong the contest. When, however, Francis had 11 to his credit and Cummings 8, it was found that the score equaled the total of the West Indian team, and the spiritedly-contested match was thus won by the Hamilton eleven, with seven wickets to the good. To the spectators the speedy disposal of the visitors in their second innings was a disappointment, as it terminated the rivalry before 5 o'clock, and until one after another of the best bats of the West Indian team capitulated before the really splendid bowling of the Hamiltonians, it was believed that the match would not terminate until close on that hour, if, indeed, it did not end in a draw. The bowling analysis demonstrates how effective the bowling on the side of the Hamiltons was.

———

The West Indian team were particularly struck by the fine appearance of Mr. Wm Hendrie's splendid team, driven tandem by Mrs. Hendrie, who graced both days' play with her presence.

The visitors are a patriarchal crowd. No fewer than three Isaacs accompanied them.

Mr. Wyatt and his team will spend a few days at Niagara Falls, the wonders of which will be gazed on for the first time by the majority of the cricketers, and then Philadelphia will be visited. While there, they will engage the leading teams, including the Young Americans and the Merion. Afterwards they will play a match with the New York cricketers on Staten Island, and will sail for home on September 24th. So far, they have been delighted with the success of their trip, and promise to come again.

The visitors were the guests of Mr. A. Bruce, Q.C., yesterday. They left by the evening train for the Falls.

Rev. Mr. Harris, of Buffalo, formerly of Jamaica, and Mr. Alex. Gartshore, of this city, umpired on Saturday.

Both teams were photographed on the grounds.

———

From the Spectator, August 28th.

Play was resumed at 3 o'clock. After a few overs Cummings retired and Gillespie replaced him, the former having been hid pretty hard. Collymore was caught neatly by Patterson off Ferrie, after he had scored 1, and Kerr went out in the next over in the same way, Patterson catching him nearly over the wicket of Gillespie's bowling. The ninth wicket fell for 73 runs. Isaacs and Swain were the last men to bat. Though the tail of the team they proved a lively tail, both batting steadily, and Swain brilliantly. Hits for twos and threes followed in quick succession, most of them made by Swain. The bowling was changed frequently—Gillespie, Cummings and Kennedy taking turns at one end, while Ferrie pegged away at the other. At last Swain gave a chance to Robertson, who accepted it. Swain and Isaacs had piled up 41 runs between them, 27 of which were contributed by Swain, a little man, but a hard and skilful hitter. The innings closed for 114.

It was 4.30 p.m. when the Hamilton team went to bat. Dr. Woolverton and Patterson were sent in first. To the bowling of Farquharson and Stewart. Patterson soon popped a ball to Farquharson who took it. Six runs had then been made, 2 of which were made by Patterson. Gillespie took his place. The score ran up quickly to 21, when Gillespie, after getting in 8 runs by several fine hits, was bowled by Farquharson, the ball cannoning off his pad into the wickets. Harvey went in, but he did not keep company with the doctor long, the latter being caught at slip by Marshall, after adding 5 to the score. The third wicket was down for 24 runs. In a minute the fourth was down for 27. Guthrie being run out by a very rash attempt to steal a run and adding nothing to the score. Cummings took his place and began immediately to drive the ball all over the field. In a few minutes he and Harvey (the latter batting very steadily and carefully) had run the score up to 46; but at this point Cummings, in endeavouring to hit hard one of Farquharson's balls, misjudged it, and it took his wickets. Ferrie was next batter, and he and Harvey played steadily for several overs without increasing the score much. When the score was 50, Harvey was caught at the wicket off Farquharson. He was replaced by Dixon, and he and Ferrie made an excellent stand, both of them batting with good judgment and so effectually, that when the stumps were drawn at 6 o'clock they had run the score up to 69.

The match will be resumed at 10 o'clock this morning. The Hamilton team has 45 runs to make in order to tie, and four wickets to fall.

The fielding of both teams yesterday was on the whole sharp and steady, though far from perfect. The visitors are all excellent batters. They will make the local Club work hard to-day.

The members of the visiting team were entertained at dinner last night at the Hamilton club by a few Hamilton cricketers and others.

———

HAMILTON, Aug. 27.—In the cricket match here to-day between the West Indians and the Hamiltons, the West Indians were all disposed of in the first innings for 114 runs. The Hamiltons had made 72 runs for six wickets when stumps were drawn at six o'clock, the seventh man not being out.

No. 7 Match.

From the Philadelphia Record, 2nd September.

West Indians v. Merion Cricket Club.

West Indians.

First Innings.

J. Lees, c Morley, b Bates 0
E. M. Skeete, c Bates, b Morley 13
E. N. Marshall, b Bates 4
W. H. Farquharson, run out 4
G. Wyatt, b Morley 0
R. H. Stewart, b Morley 6
L. L. Kerr, c Etting, b Morley 1
L. Fyfe, c Haines, b Morley 0
J. M. Burke, not out 10
L. Isaacs, c Philler, b Lowry 5
A. Swain, c Haines, b Morley 4
Extras............................... 7
Total.............................. 54

Second Innings.

J. Lees, c Haines, b Morley 3
E. M. Skeete, b Lowry 7
E. N. Marshall, b Morley 2
W. H. Farquharson, c Haines, b Morley 11
G. Wyatt, c Law, b Lowry 0
R. H. Stewart, c Haines, b Lowry 3
L. L. Kerr, not out 1
L. Fyfe, c Lowry, b Morley 0
J. M. Burke, b Law 2
L. Isaacs, c Philler, b Lowry 1
A. Swain, b Lowry 5
Extras 1
Total.............................. 36

Merion.

First Innings.

W. E. Bates, c Kerr, b Farquharson 0
C.S. Edwards, c Kerr, b Burke 2
N. Etting, run out 3
Morley, c Isaacs, b Burke 13
A. G. Thompson, c Kerr, b Farquharson 2
S. Law, b Farquharson 7
A. C. Craig, b Farquharson 14
B. Henry, c Kerr, b Burke 2
G. S. Philler, not out 26
C. E. Haines, b Farquharson 0
W. C. Lowry, b Burke 13
Extras 4
Total 86

Second Innings.

C. S. Edwards, not out 2
A. C. Craig, not out 0
Extras 4
Total 6

BOWLING ANALYSIS.

WEST INDIANS.

First Innings.

	Balls	Mdns.	Rns.	Wkts.
Bates	56	8	15	2
Morley	83	10	17	6
Law	16	1	7	0
Lowry	12	7	8	1

Second Innings.

	Balls	Mdns.	Rns.	Wkts.
Morley	52	7	15	4
Lowry	64	5	18	5
Law	16	3	2	1

MERION.

First Innings.

	Balls	Mdns.	Rns.	Wkts.
Burke	81	7	46	4
Farquharson	80	2	36	5

Second Innings.

	Balls	Mdns.	Rns.	Wkts.
Burke	8	1	1	0
Farquharson	8	1	1	0

Farquharson bowled 1 wide.

RUNS AT THE FALL OF EACH WICKET.

First Innings.

West Indians	0	6	13	13	25	30	31	31	44	54
Merion	2	2	10	13	27	36	41	53	53	86

Second Innings.

West Indians	6	11	13	13	27	30	30	30	30	36

VICTORY AND DEFEAT.—TWO GAMES BY THE WEST INDIAN CRICKETERS AT ARDMORE.

When stumps were drawn on Tuesday evening in the match between the West Indian cricketers and the Merion Club, at Ardmore, the result was doubtful, notwithstanding the fact that the visitors, with one wicket down in their second innings, were 21 runs to the bat. It was generally concluded they had played in hard luck, and everyone expected to see them make a good showing yesterday. The wicket had greatly improved, and was rather more favourable to batsmen than otherwise. Contrary to all anticipations, however, the morning's cricket was disappointing, the visitors only increasing their total from 11 to 36. This left Merion but 5 runs to make to win, and the requisite number was obtained without loss, compelling the West Indians to accept a defeat by ten wickets.

L. R. Fyfe

From the Philadelphia Inquirer, 2nd September.

The cricket match between the West Indian team and the first eleven of the Merion Club which was begun at Ardmore on Tuesday, was brought to an abrupt termination yesterday morning. Although the condition of the ground had greatly improved from a batsman's point of view, the visitors failed to take advantage of it and with nine wickets to fall in their second innings, they only succeeded in adding twenty-five runs to their over-night total eleven. As the home team held a lead of thirty-two at the end of the first game, they only required five runs to win, and these were obtained easily without loss, the players from the tropics having to acknowledge defeat by ten wickets.

No. 8 MATCH.

From the Philadelphia Record, 2nd September.

MERION.

C. S. Edwards, c Fyfe, b Burke 13
A. C. Craig, b Farquharson 1
W. E. Bates, b Farquharson 0
C. Morris, b Farquharson 8
Morley, b Farquharson 0
A. G. Thompson, b Farquharson 2
S. Law, b Burke. 16
G. S. Philler, b Lees 7
B. Henry, not out 13
C. E. Haines, b Lees 15
W. C. Lowry, c Kerr, b Burke 20
Extras 12
Total. 107

WEST INDIANS.

J. Lees, not out 40
E. M. Skeete, c Haines, b Morley 28
L. Kerr, c Henry, b Lowry 12
E. N. Marshall, c Morris, b Lowry 0
W. H. Farquharson, c Bates, b Morley 13
R. H. Stewart, st. Haines, b Lowry 6
G. Wyatt, c Bates, b Lowry 7
Extras 5
Total. 111

BOWLING ANALYSIS.

MERION.

	Balls	Mdns.	Rns.	Wkts.
Burke	109	13	37	3
Farquharson	68	9	19	5
Lees	28	0	25	2
Stewart	12	0	14	0

WEST INDIANS.

	Balls	Mdns.	Rns.	Wkts.
Thompson	12	1	7	0
Craig	20	1	7	0
Lowry	97	4	51	4
Edwards	16	1	5	0
Law	56	9	14	0
Morley	68	9	22	2

RUNS AT THE FALL OF EACH WICKET.

Merion............ .8	14	16	16	22	31	61	55	77	107
West Indians.......... 49	70	70	91	92	111				

———

THE RETURN MATCH.

As the match terminated at a very early hour it was decided to play a return game, which was started at 12.45 o'clock with the home team at the bat. It soon became evident that the West Indians were on their mettle, and before dinner was announced, half of the Merion wickets had been lost for 22 runs. Upon resuming, however, a decided improvement took place, and the innings realized the respectable total of 107. Lowry, Law, Haines and Henry, who scored 20, 16, 15 and 13 not out, being the principal contributors. The batting essay of the visitors was auspiciously opened by Lees and Skeete, and as several of their colleagues gave adequate assistance the team were enabled to claim the victory with four wickets to spare, thus making matters even with their first Philadelphia opponents.

———

From the Philadelphia Inquirer, 2nd September.

As the day was young a second match was immediately started, Merion being first to the bat. Farquharson and Burke, the premier bowlers of the West Indian eleven, evinced a retaliatory spirit, and when the dinner bell sounded, five of the opposing team had been dismissed for the insignificant total of 22. The tail end, however, played up pluckily, Lowry, Law, Haines and Henry showing to good advantage, and the venture produced an aggregate of 107. Whatever adverse criticism may have been evoked on the run-getting capabilities of the visitors by their previous doings was quickly recalled, as Lees, and Skeete, the first pair to handle the willow, instantly settled down to earnest work. Runs came apace, notwithstanding the changes of bowling, and before the separation was effected, the score was within one of the half century. Kerr and Farquharson also batted well, but Lees, who carried his bat for forty, gave a masterly exhibition of scientific cricket, and fairly earned the applause with which he was greeted at the end of the game. Time was called shortly after the winning hit was made, and the visiting cricketers left the ground with the consolation that they had made matters square with their genial hosts.

No. 9 Match.

From the Philadelphia Press, 4th September.

West Indians v. Belmont c. c.

West Indians.

First Innings.		*Second Innings.*	
E. M. Skeete, c Colladay, b W. Scott	0	E. M. Skeete, b W. Scott	0
J. Lees, c J. A. Scott, b Bradley	25	J. Lees, c Coates, b W. Scott	40
P. Isaacs, b W. Scott	1	P. Isaacs, c Wright, b Colladay	1
R. H. Stewart, c Stiles, b W. Scott	9	R. H. Stewart, c Mackin, b W. Scott	7
W. H. Farquharson, c Work, b W. Scott	5	W. H. Farquharson, c Smith, b W. Scott	2
G. Wyatt, c J. A. Scott, b Bradley	1	G. Wyatt, not out	33
L. Fyfe, c Bradley, b W. Scot	8	L. Fyfe, c Colladay, b Bradley	3
J. M. Burke, st. J. A. Scott, b W. Scott	7	J. M. Burke, c Wood, b Colladay	3
T. Skeete, c Wright, b Bradley	1	T. Skeete, c Colladay, b W. Scott	5
L. Isaacs, b Wood	13	L. Isaacs, c Bradley, b Wright	2
W. Collymore, not out	3	W. Collymore, c Bradley, b W. Scott	12
Extras	1	Extras	8
Total	74	Total	116

Belmont Club.

J. A. Scott, b Farquharson	77
M. C. Work, st P. Isaacs, b Lees	10
W. Scott, b Burke	8
A. Machin, c Stewart, b Burke	8
F. Walters, c P Isaacs, b Burke	25
Bradley, c Burke, b Farquharson	1
M. D. Smith, run out	31
C. Coates, c Stewart, b Burke	4
S. Wood, b L. Isaacs	15
W. T. Wright, b Farquharson	14
S. R. Colladay, not out	9
Extras	20
Total	222

BOWLING ANALYSIS.

WEST INDIANS.

First Innings.	Balls	Mds.	Rns.	Wkts.
W. Scott	112	9	27	6
Colladay	48	8	11	0
Bradley	76	7	24	3
Wood	29	2	11	1

Colladay bowled 1 wide.

Second Innings.	Balls	Mds.	Rns.	Wkts.
W. Scott	127	18	23	6
Colladay	88	13	16	2
Wood	44	7	10	0
Coates	36	3	17	0
Machin	24	3	5	0
Bradley	52	7	18	1
Smith	24	2	5	0
Wright	48	6	14	1

Colladay bowled 3 wides. Wood bowled 1 no-ball.

BELMONT.

	Balls	Mds.	Rns.	Wkts.
Burke	183	15	77	4
Farquharson	92	6	36	3
Lees	88	7	38	1
Stewart	48	3	23	0
T. Skeete	8	0	6	0
L. Isaacs	48	3	22	1

RUNS AT THE FALL OF EACH WICKET.

First Innings.

West Indians	0	5	23	33	41	42	51	52	71	74
Belmont	32	54	87	120	137	141	151	188	188	222

Second Innings.

West Indians	3	5	16	18	41	66	79	81	87	116

The second day's play of the match between the visiting cricketers from the West Indies and the Belmont Club was began yesterday morning at an early hour.

On Thursday afternoon when the stumps were drawn at 4 o'clock the score stood for one innings each: West Indians 74 and 222, leaving the islands 140 runs in the rear. They were not dismayed at the magnitude of the work ahead of them and sent Lees and E. Skeete to combat the bowling of Walter Scott and Colladay. As usual Skeete was the first unfortunate victim being retired by a beauty from Scott. P. Isaacs did not remain for any length of time to give a material help to Lees, who was handling the willow very carefully and increasing his score by singles. No stand was made until Stewart and Collymore were of some service in holding up their ends while Lees added to the credit on the books of his team. The downfall of the last named redoubtable batsman was due to an excellent catch by Coates, which wound up his career when he was well set with Wyatt, and they promised at one time to give the Belmont fielders a fair exercise in leather-hunting.

Lees' score of 40 was made when the figures of his side stood at 79. A very good exhibit of batting was that shown by Wyatt, who successfully resisted all attacks of the local bowling department and carried out his bat for 33. The Elmwood players were in fine trim, but were somewhat exercised over the stand made by Lees and Wyatt, and to counteract the effect the captain had eight men to handle the ball, changing them frequently during the West Indians' second innings. The character of the efforts made is shown in the fact that 143 balls were required to cause the fall of 10 wickets for 108 runs from the bat, and that the bowling was not bad is further evinced by the 54 maiden overs played by the batsmen without adding to their credit on the score book. When the tenth wicket went down the game was the Belmont's by one innings with 32 runs to spare.

The visitors will play the Germantown strong eleven to-day on the famous international grounds at Nicetown.

———

From the Philadelphia Record, 4th September.

THE WEST INDIAN CRICKETERS BEATEN BY AN INNINGS AND 32 RUNS.

The match between the West Indian cricketers and the first eleven of the Belmont Club was brought to a conclusion yesterday at Elmwood, and resulted in a victory for the home team by one innings and 32 runs. At the close of the first day's play, the visitors had scored 74 runs for one innings, with 222 to the credit of Belmont. The sturdy cricketers from the West Indian Islands could only bring their second essay at the bat up to 116, a total in their two efforts of 120. Lees who has a strong defence and good hitting powers, obtained 40, and Wyatt followed him closely with 33, while Collymore played well for 12. W. Scott again bowled splendidly, and, being well supported by the fielders, captured six wickets at the small cost of 23 runs.

To-day and Monday the West Indian team will meet the Germantown Club at Nicetown.

From the Philadelphia Times, 4th September.

When the last wicket fell of the West Indian cricket team at Elmwood yesterday afternoon, the Belmont Club was the winner of the match by an innings and 32 runs. The visitors scored 116 runs in their second innings, but Captain Scott was evidently experimenting with his bowling strength, as he tried eight men in all. W. Scott and Colladay obtained eight wickets for 52 runs, while the other six bowlers only got two for 56 runs. Lees and Wyatt batted in good form, but the others only made 35 among them.

No. 10 Match.

From the Philadelphia Inquirer, 6th & 7th September.

West Indians v. Germantown.

Germantown.

G. S. Patterson, b Farquharson 65
W. C. Morgan, Jr., run out 85
F. W. Ralston, Jr., b Farquharson 30
A. Jessup, c Wyatt, b Burke 1
R. A. Morgan, b Farquharson 12
W. J. Duhring, b Farquharson 14
E. Comfort, b Farquharson 26
S. H. Carpenter, b Marshall 6
C. L. Kurtz, c Kerr, b Farquharson 12
S. M. Waln, run out 4
W. Brockie, Jr., not out 30
Extras 25
Total 310

West Indians.

First Innings.		*Second Innings.*	
G. Wyatt, b Duhring 0		G. Wyatt, l b w, b Patterson 3	
R. H. Stewart, b Jessup 9		R. H. Stewart, b Brockie 17	
E. M. Skeete, not out 18		E. M. Skeete, b Comfort 3	
J. Lees, b Duhring 18		J. Lees, b Comfort 37	
L. Fyfe, b Patterson 2		L. Fyfe, c Duhring, b Patterson 4	

WEST INDIANS. *(cont'd)*

First Innings.	
W. H. Farquharson, st W. C. Morgan,	
b Patterson	1
E. N. Marshall, c W. C. Morgan,	
b Duhring	1
L. L. Kerr, b Patterson	1
J. M. Burke, c Ralston, b Patterson	2
L. Isaacs, b Patterson	1
A. Swain, b Duhring	6
Extras	15
Total	74

Second Innings.	
W. H. Farquharson, b Waln	48
E. N. Marshall, c Duhring, b Patterson	16
L. L. Kerr, b Comfort	5
J. M. Burke, b Patterson	0
L. Isaacs, not out	2
A. Swain, b Comfort	0
Extras	13
Total	148

BOWLING ANALYSIS.

GERMANTOWN.

	Balls	Mdns.	Rns.	Wkts.
Burke	112	10	60	1
Farquharson	158	22	56	6
Swain	100	10	46	0
Lees	108	10	57	0
Marshall	36	1	25	1
Isaacs	12	1	8	0
Stewart	72	4	33	0

Burke bowled 2 wides.

WEST INDIANS.

First Innings.				
	Balls	Mdns.	Rns.	Wkts.
Duhring	112	17	24	4
Patterson	156	26	20	5
Jessup	44	6	15	1

Wides—Duhring, 2; Jessup 2. Duhring bowled
1 no-ball.

Second Innings.				
	Balls.	Mdns.	Rns.	Wkts.
Comfort	129	14	62	4
W. C. Morgan, Jr.	36	6	9	0
Patterson	108	15	23	4
R. A. Morgan	64	6	25	0
Waln	56	6	6	1
Brockie	32	6	5	1
Duhring	12	1	5	0

Wides—Waln, 2; Brockie, 2; Duhring, 2.
No-balls—Patterson, 1; R.A. Morgan, 1;
Duhring, 1.

RUNS AT THE FALL OF EACH WICKET.

First Innings.

Germantown 167	183	186	210	228	231	240	257	265	310	
West Indians 2	20	42	49	50	51	53	59	64	74	

Second Innings.

West Indians. 13	46	96	103	119	130	144	146	146	148	

———

CRICKETERS FROM THE TROPICS IN PHILADELPHIA.

The cricketers from the West Indies have not been successful in Philadelphia thus far. In fact, they have made a somewhat indifferent showing. Against a rather weak eleven of Merion they were beaten by ten wickets, owing to remarkably feeble batting in their second innings. A "return" match at Ardmore, played to fill in time, they won, and won so creditably, that every one was prepared to see them make stubborn fights with the other clubs. Their defeat by Belmont, however, was even more decisive than their first reverse, and on Saturday, at Nicetown, they were compelled to hunt leather for many long hours. Nevertheless, the aggregation is a good one, and understanding the conditions of their visit, it is not a difficult matter to account for their poor work against the strong organizations they have met in this city. In the first place many of the players were strangers to each other until they came together at Montreal, and consequently the captain of the team has had to rely solely on the reputations of the men previously unknown to him. By this time, of course, he is in a position to judge of the capabilities of his players, and is able to work them to advantage, but for all that they can be no match in team work for such well-disciplined elevens as are found in and around this city. Furthermore, the islanders are not accustomed to American wickets, their own being harder, rougher and faster. Again, they are under too great a strain. They play cricket day after day, and generally spend their evening in enjoying the hospitality of their hosts.

These are the principal reasons why they have failed to do themselves justice. The result of the five days' play here shows that J. Lees is by far and away the best all-round man. He is, without doubt, first class, and is worthy of a place on almost any eleven. W. H. Farquharson and J. M. Burke are fair average bowlers, and the same might be said of E. N. Marshall. Generally speaking, however, the team is deficient in bowling talent, and were it not for good, steady fielding, the scores against them would be larger than they are. To sum up, the visitors are playing under many disadvantages, but, making every allowance possible, it is clear that they are not up to the form of the leading local clubs.

THE WEST INDIANS AT NICETOWN.

The two-days' match between the first eleven of the Germantown Club and the cricketers from the West Indies was begun at Nicetown on Saturday in presence of a large attendance. The home captain having won the toss assigned his opponents' duty in the field and sent in Patterson and W. C. Morgan, Jnr. to resist the attack of Burke and Farquharson. Those who delight in seeing scientific batting had every reason to be satisfied with the exhibition which followed the call of "play." The two young cricketers, despite many changes of bowling, maintained their positions all the morning and for a portion of the afternoon. Patterson finally succumbing to Farquharson, after contributing 65 to a total of 167. Morgan, who made 85, did not long survive his companion, being unfortunately run out when he lacked but 15 runs of the century. The troubles of the visitors did not terminate with the downfall of the first pair, as Ralston, R. A. Morgan, Duhring, Comfort, Kurtz and Brockie also scored freely, and when the last wicket fell the register showed that the team had put together the large aggregate of 310. The West Indians began batting about 5 o'clock, and when time was called had obtained 34 for the loss of two wickets. The match will be resumed today at eleven o'clock.

WEST INDIAN VISITORS DEFEATED BY THE GERMANTOWN ELEVEN.

As anticipated, yesterday's play in the two day's match between the cricketers from the West Indies and the first eleven of the Germantown Club, at Nicetown, resulted in the defeat of the visitors by a decisive margin. When stumps were drawn on Saturday evening, the home team had completed their first innings for 310, and their opponents had lost two wickets for a total of 34 runs. It was, therefore, thought that the local champion would be satisfied with nothing short of an innings victory, which they finally achieved, with 88 runs to spare.

Upon resuming operations, Skeete and Lees, who were not out with 4 and 12 respectively, were faced by Duhring and Patterson, and only 8 runs had been added to the score when the fast bowler got rid of the West Indian "crack" who had placed 18 to his credit. His departure was followed by a succession of disasters, which only ended with the close of the innings. Skeete continued to play in his careful manner throughout, but could get no one to stay with him. At 49 Captain Fyfe succumbed to Patterson, and one run later Farquharson was stumped by the agile Morgan. Marshall, the next comer, was caught at the wicket off Duhring after contributing a single, and at 53 the slow trundler responded by upsetting Kerr's pegs. Burke followed, but he failed to stay, being caught by Ralston off Patterson at 59. Isaacs fared no better, as after making one of the next five runs booked, he likewise fell a victim to Patterson's insidious deliveries. Swain brought up the rear and closed the innings by failing to stop a straight one from Duhring.

As the essay only realized 74, the West Indians were compelled to follow on, and, after dinner had been discussed, Farquharson and Skeete were sent in to resist the attack of Comfort and W. C. Morgan, Jr. The deficit having been reduced by 13, Skeete was sent back by Comfort, but the partnership of Farquharson and Stewart was more productive, and it was not until 36 had been added that Brockie, who had just taken the ball, succeeded in dislodging the last comer for 17. Lees then joined the giant of the team, and for a time the Germantown men were given a taste of leather hunting. Both batsmen hit hard and clean, and, although the bowling was frequently changed, the pair remained in company until, with the aggregate of 96, Farquharson, who had shown sound cricket for 48, was bowled by Waln.

The century appeared on the telegraph board shortly after the arrival of Captain Fyfe, who, however, had to leave at 103, a catch by Duhring at point off Patterson being the cause of his departure. Wyatt then joined Lees, but the alliance was not of long duration, as, with 119 chronicled, the latter dismissed by Comfort for a superbly gathered 37. Marshall lost the companionship of Wyatt at 130, that gallant defender having been given out, l. b. w., on Patterson's appeal. Kerr, who filled the gap, met with an accident soon after making his appearance, and temporarily retired, his place being taken by Burke. Marshall's turn to leave came next, his lively innings of 16 being terminated by Duhring, who caught him at point at 144. Burke, Swain, and Kerr were bowled by Comfort in the order named, the venture closing for 148.

No. 11 Match.

West Indians v. Young America.—Played at Philadelphia on
7th and 8th Sept., 1886.

West Indians.

First Innings.		Second Innings.	
E. M. Skeete, c Schwartz, b Brewster	2	E. M. Skeete, c & b Brewster	11
W. H. Farquharson, c Downs, b Brewster	6	W. H. Farquharson, b Brewster	4
R. H. Stewart, c Downs, b C. A. Newhall	8	R. H. Stewart, b C. A. Newhall	3
J. Lees, b C. A. Newhall	33	J. Lees, c Patterson, b Brewster	37
P. Isaacs, b Clark	13	P. Isaacs, c Clark, b Brewster	16
G. Wyatt, c R. S. Newhall, b Brewster	0	G. Wyatt, b Brewster	64
E. N. Marshall, b Brewster	1	E. N. Marshall, b Brewster	14
W. Collymore, b Clark	1	J. M. Burke, not out	6
J. M. Burke, not out	10	L. Fyfe, not out	6
T. Skeete, c Dixon, b Brewster	1	Extras	14
L. Fyfe, c Clarke, b C. A. Newhall	1	Total	175
Extras	13		
Total	89		

Young America.

F. E. Brewster, l b w, b Marshall	70
N. Downs, b Lees	12
R. S. Newhall, c Farquharson, b Burke	83
C. A. Newhall, run out	31
T. H. Dixon, c Lees, b Burke	8
E. W. Clark, Jr., b Farquharson	28
J. H. Patterson, c Wyatt, b Burke	5
H. L. Brown, b Stewart	34
H. H. Firth, st Wyatt, b Stewart	0
E. H. Hance, Jr., not out	5
A. F. Schwartz, st Wyatt, b Stewart	0
Extras	8
Total	284

BOWLING ANALYSIS.

West Indians.

First Innings.

	Balls	Mdns.	Rns.	Wkts.
C.A. Newhall	114	15	25	3
Brewster	152	23	23	5
Clark	64	7	25	2
Firth	34	4	3	0

Clark bowled 1 wide.

Second Innings.

	Balls	Mdns.	Rns.	Wkts.
C.A. Newhall	136	17	40	1
Brewster	168	17	62	6
Clark	68	6	31	0
Downs	12	1	6	0
Firth	44	4	13	0
Brown	12	1	9	0

Firth bowled 1 wide, and Downs 1 no-ball.

Young America.

	Balls	Mdns.	Rns.	Wkts.
Burke	200	23	71	3
Farquharson	184	12	94	1
Lees	120	7	64	1
Marshall	68	9	24	1
Stewart	30	1	23	3

Runs at the Fall of Each Wicket.

First Innings.

West Indians	3	16	18	55	56	59	62	81	86	89
Young America	62	110	199	199	210	229	267	277	278	284

Second Innings.

West Indians	15	31	34	39	135	161	162

THE WEST INDIANS AT STENTON.

The cricketers from the West Indies put in an appearance yesterday morning on the grounds of the Young America Club at Stenton in their usual cheerful mood to play the fourth game of their series with local clubs. Though disaster attended their efforts in the three previous matches with the Merion, the Belmont and the Germantown Clubs, it seemed to have no effect upon their play at the bat or in the field. Each man yesterday, as the champions of 1885 punished the bowling, appeared to be endowed with renewed strength and ambition. The attendance was somewhat slim and it was mainly confined to carriage parties, who, after a brief stay, and upon hearing that the Young

America men were doing quite well, drove to other and more interesting pursuits, as lawn tennis was a forbidden pleasure when the first eleven are on the ground.

Shortly before noon E. M. Skeete and Farquharson appeared at the wickets, with C. A. Newhall and Brewster to conduct offensive operations for Young America. Skeete retired first, leaving Stewart in his place. No stand was made until Lees and Isaacs brought the score to 55, and shortly afterwards the first-named batsman, who has uniformly contributed double figures in each innings played by him, was clean bowled by a beauty from the "Grand Old Man." Isaacs 13 and Burke with 10, not out, were the only other men to swell the score by more than one figure. The innings terminated at 89.

Brewster and Downs then wielded the willow for Young America, and with good effect, especially on the part of Brewster, whose cutting was a grand exhibit of scientific cricket. The runs were piled up in quick order, no less than 62 runs being had from the bat in 59 minutes, when Downs, who patiently defended his stumps for a nice 12, fell to a good one from Lees. Robert S. Newhall was next and brought the score to 110 with some of his old-time hard hitting by drives and cuts. At this point Brewster's leg got before the wicket, and Charles Newhall succeeded him. The brothers rapidly advanced the score in the next hour to 169, when time was called, Charles getting a grand leg hit to the clubhouse for 5.

The match will be resumed this morning. The visiting team was entertained last evening at the Wissahickon Inn by the hospitable men of Germantown and Young America.

———

A DRAW AT CRICKET.

The West Indians cricket team have had one satisfaction in their local series of games, inasmuch as they pulled off a draw yesterday with the Young America Club at Stenton. It was a slight concession to the visitors, but it filled them with pride, and they left the city last evening to play at Boston, better pleased than they have felt at the result of the three previous games. The West Indians only made 89 during their first essay at the bat, while the Young America men gave the scorers the trouble of recording 284 runs as their contribution. The second innings of the visitors was not at first marked with much spirit, as four men were out for only 39 runs. Wyatt and the inevitable Lees were then in partnership, and did a very profitable business at the local team's expense, Wyatt, especially forcing his credit by hard hitting and good cricket to 64 before his stumps dropped to one of Brewster's slows. Lees was first out, though, at 135 for the fifth wicket, while Wyatt stayed until seventh wicket down for 162. The visitors were playing for a draw, and they succeeded in obtaining their object, though the game, had it been played to an end, would have resulted in a substantial victory for the Young America.

No. 12 Match.

From the Boston Daily Globe, 10th & 11th September.

West Indians v. Longwoods.—Played at Boston on

10th and 11th Sept., 1886.

West Indians.

First Innings.		Second Innings.	
E. M. Skeete, c L. Mansfield, b Hubbard ... 31		E. M. Skeete, c Brown, b G. Wright 1	
R. H. Stewart, b Chambers 9		R. H. Stewart, c Brown, b Chambers 0	
W. H. Farquharson, b Chambers 0		W. H. Farquharson, b Chambers 0	
J. Lees, not out 34		J. Lees, c Brown, b Wright 0	
G. Wyatt, c G. Wright, b Hubbard 4		G. Wyatt, b Chambers 4	
L. Fyfe, c Chambers, b Hubbard 1		L. Fyfe, c Brown, b Wright 0	
L. L. Kerr, c L. Mansfield, b Hubbard 1		L. L. Kerr, b Chambers 6	
W. Collymore, c. S. Wright, b Chambers 8		W. Collymore, b Chambers 1	
J. M. Burke, c L. Mansfield, b G. Wright 1		J. M. Burke, c Dutton, b Chambers 3	
L. A. Isaacs, b Chambers 0		L. A. Isaacs, b Chambers 3	
A. Swain, b Chambers 0		A. Swain, b Chambers 0	
T. Skeete, c G. Wright, b Chambers 2		T. Skeete, not out 19	
Extras 6		Extras 2	
Total 97		Total 39	

Longwoods.

First Innings.		Second Innings.	
L. Mansfield, b Stewart 7		L. Mansfield, b Burke 0	
C. L. Bixby, b Stewart 8		C. L. Bixby, c Kerr, b Burke 0	
J. G. Hubbard, b Stewart 2		J. G. Hubbard, st Kerr, b Stewart 2	
C. U. Stuart, c Kerr, b Stewart 2		C. U. Stuart, c Fyfe, b Stewart 3	
H. P. McKean, c Kerr, b Farquharson 37		H. P. McKean, b Burke 0	
Sam Wright, c Isaacs, b Stewart 5		Sam Wright, b Burke 1	
I. Chambers, c Wyatt, b Burke 6		I Chambers, b Burke 0	
Geo. Wright, st Kerr, b Lees 8		Geo. Wright, st Kerr, b Stewart 8	

LONGWOODS. *(cont'd)*

First Innings.		Second Innings.	
F. A. Appleton, c Fyfe, b Farquharson. 6		F. A. Appleton, absent . . . . o	
J. W. Dutton, not out. 4		J. W. Dutton, st Kerr, b Stewart 2	
F. S. Mansfield, c Kerr, b Lees. 2		F. S. Mansfield, not out 2	
C. A. Brown, c & b Lees . . . . o		C. A. Brown, l b w, b Burke 1	
Extras. 8		Extras. 4	
Total. 95		Total. 23	

BOWLING ANALYSIS.

WEST INDIANS.

First Innings.	Balls	Mdns.	Rns.	Wkts.	Second Innings.	Balls	Mdns.	Rns.	Wkts.
G. Wright 80		12	13	1	G. Wright 96		13	20	3
Chambers. 192		25	39	6	Chambers 94		17	17	8
Bixby. 12		0	12	0					
Hubbard. 93		15	27	4					

LONGWOODS.

First Innings.	Balls	Mdns.	Rns.	Wkts.	Second Innings.	Balls	Mdns.	Rns.	Wkts.
Burke. 100		13	28	1	Burke. 52		9	7	6
Stewart. 104		10	40	5	Stewart. 48		7	12	4
Farquharson. 68		9	16	2					
Lees 19		2	5	3					

RUNS AT THE FALL OF EACH WICKET.

First Innings.

West Indians 30	40	44	52	62	64	86	88	89	89	97
Longwoods. 15	19	24	33	45	59	77	89	89	95	95

Second Innings.

West Indians . . . . o	2	2	2	3	6	12	12	14	19	39
Longwoods 2	4	4	4	4	4	13	14	22	23	

OPENING OF THE MATCH AT LONGWOOD.

Owing to the disagreeable weather, the cricket visitors from the West Indies did not arrive on the Longwood grounds until some minutes after noon, and after winning the toss, Captain Fyfe decided to take advantage of the promising wicket, and sent his men to the bat. E. M. Skeete and R. H. Stewart went to the defence at 12.40. George Wright opening the bowling from the Pavilion end, and started with a maiden. Chambers took the ball at the lower wicket, and his first ball was sent by Stewart to leg for three, and his partner followed with a single. Wright followed with a maiden, and on Chamber's next over, a close thing on run out was in order. Wright bowled another maiden, which Chambers duplicated. Skeete then cut Wright for 3, and Chambers sent down another maiden over. Stewart here made a pretty drive to the on for 2. At 12, both men batting very steadily, Bixby went on in place of Wright, and his last ball was hit to forward cover for 3. The first ball of Chamber's next over shared a like fate at leg, sent there by the same batsman. Skeete here put Bixby to the off for 3, which brought up 20. Brown here missed an easy chance of stumping Stewart off Chambers, and that batter improved the opportunity by cutting Bixby for 3; which his partner duplicated. Skeete then got a single off Chambers, but lost his partner the same over; he retired from a "yorker" from the professional. W. H. Farquharson now joined Skeete, and the latter played Hubbard, who had relieved Bixby, for a 3, and scored another 3 at leg off the professional. This brought up 49 on the board, and only one wicket down. Chambers then retired Farquharson, and J. Lees filled the vacancy. The latter played a fine defensive game, the bowling at both ends being well on, until Skeete was easily taken at point by L. Mansfield off Hubbard, after a splendid innings of 31, compiled by grand play, and without giving the shadow of a chance during the fifty minutes he was at bat, and having in his score 8 three-hits. Three for 44. Guy Wyatt was next man, and runs now came very slowly, as Chambers had bowled 9 maidens out of 18 overs, while Hubbard's record was 11 overs, 8 maidens, 7 of which were consecutive ones. Wyatt, after playing rather timidly at first, opened his scoring with a 3 to leg off Hubbard. Fifty was now up, and the prospects for a very even game were decidedly promising. After showing considerable steady play, Wyatt gave a hard chance to G. Wright at forward cover-point, which was taken very low down. Four for 52. Captain Fyfe followed in, and played steady defence, while his partner scored in good shape, his hits to leg being in fine form, until the captain was neatly secured by Chambers off Hubbard. Five for 62. Lunch was then announced.

Play was resumed at 11 o'clock this morning with the not-outs, McKean and Sam Wright, at the bat; Burke opening with the ball at the lower wicket,

Sam taking the opening ball, and scoring 1, but after scoring another single, he was caught by Isaacs off Stewart. Five for 45. Chambers joined McKean who was batting prettily, but after registering two 3's, he was well caught at coverpoint by Wyatt, off Stewart. Six for 59. George Wright now joined McKean, and the latter did most of the scoring for a considerable time, hitting and driving for 2's and 3's. Seventy was now up, and Longwood stock rising. McKean now hit Stewart over the fence for 4, and cut the next ball for 2. Burke bowled down another maiden; Farquharson then relieved Stewart at the club-house wicket and started with a maiden which Burke duplicated, and in Farquharson's next over McKean was finely caught at the wicket, having, so far, the top score of the match, 37, which contained two 4's, four 3's, five 2's, and singles—a brilliant innings, carefully played. Seven for 77. Appleton now joined George Wright, who had commenced to score in his usual manner, sending Farquharson to the mid boundary for 4, and after two overs of steady playing, Appleton started with a square leg-hit for a like number off the other bowler. Farquharson had now bowled 6 overs, 4 maidens for 1 wicket and 4 runs. At 88 Lees went on in place of Burke, and on his first over Wright was grandly stumped by Kerr. Eight for 89. Sutton was next man, but he immediately lost Appleton, who was splendidly caught by the genial captain, off Farquharson's bowling, without the score changing. Dutton here cut Lees to the ropes for 4, and F. Mansfield, who now partnered him, after giving a very hard chance to short slip, drove for 2, which brought the total to 95, or two behind the visitors' total, but he was soon caught at the wicket off the slow bowler. Brown was last man in, and the fielders worked in grand style to retain the lead on the first innings, which was eventually accomplished by Lees catching the last-comer off his own bowling. All out for 95, and thus lacking 2 of the total of the visitors. A close thing for all concerned, as time now (12.15) will hardly permit of the game being played out, although, should the Longwoods field in anything near their usual brilliant manner the West Indians should be disposed of by about 3 o'clock, which then would give time to the home team to capture the game.

The West Indians went to the bat for their second innings at 12.25, E. M. Skeete and Stewart going to the defence, but almost immediately the last-named was caught by Browne off Chambers, and on Wright's next over that wicket-keeper also secured Skeete. One for 0, and two for 2. This was well supplemented by Chambers's bowling the new-comer, Collymore, without the score changing, and Dutton here missed a chance of retiring a batter at short-leg, but a few balls after, Brown again distinguished himself by securing Lees (who had scored so brilliantly in the first innings), and all but had Farquharson, the same over. Four for 2 runs, and the bowling at both ends not to be hit. Five overs (4 maidens), 2 wickets to Chambers. Five wickets for 3 runs! Is this a "rot" set in, or only the proverbial chances of wicket? 12.55.— Guy Wyatt, the promoter of the tour, and Captain Fyfe are together, and both the bowlers are sending down maidens. Wyatt here broke the monotony by sending G. Wright to leg for 3. Ten maiden overs for Chambers, out of eleven bowled, with four wickets for 1 run. Wright is not far behind with 9 maidens out of 11 overs, with 2 wickets for 5 runs. Wyatt retires. Six for 6 runs. Kerr fills the vacancy. One more maiden for Wright, and a 2 to the off breaks Chambers's long string of maiden overs, and a 3 by Kerr off Wright followed, and the same batter hit Chambers for 2. Two more maidens from Chambers, and on the third from Wright, Brown again distinguishes himself by retiring the captain. Seven for 12. Burke follows in, but the next ball from Chambers sends Kerr to the club house. Eight for 12. T. Skeete was next man, and after playing steady cricket some six overs, he hit Wright for 5; and the next ball, Burke cut for 3; but the latter was finely caught by Dutton off Chambers the next over: nine for 19. Swain was next man in, and out: ten for 19. L. L. Isaacs brought up the rear. Skeete hit Wright to leg for 2, and after another maiden from Chambers, cut Wright to the ropes and afterwards hit Chambers to the leg for 3 and repeated this the following over, but his partner lost his wicket to the professional, and all were out at 1.55 for 39 runs. Chambers's record is indeed very brilliant. This leaves the Longwoods 42 runs to get to win.

———

From the Boston Herald, 12th September.

DEFEAT OF LONGWOOD CRICKETERS BY 18 RUNS.—REMARKABLY FINE AVERAGES ON BOTH SIDES.

The match between the team of gentlemen cricketers from the British West Indian Islands and the Longwood club, which was commenced on Friday under unfavourable weather auspices, was brought to a close yesterday afternoon on the Longwood grounds in the presence of a large company, and resulted in victory for the foreigners by 18 runs, to the great astonishment of the victors as well as the spectators. In the first innings of the visitors, which was closed on Friday, they made 97 runs, and that of the home team, which commenced on Friday and closed shortly after noon yesterday, resulted in a score of 95. The visitors then commenced their second innings, and at the very outset something like a panic seemed to have seized them, as the first five wickets fell for six runs, and at the fall of the last wicket but one, only 19 were up on the telegraph board, but the steady batting and hard hitting of T. Skeete ran up the score to 39 before his partner's wicket fell. An hour was then devoted for luncheon, when the Longwoods went to the bat with the expectation that not more than four or five men would be needed to get the 42 runs required to win the match, but it soon became evident that what looked like a panic in the visitors' second innings was a real one in that of the Longwoods as the first six wickets fell for only 4 runs, and the eight for only 14, and as Appleton, from whom a good score was expected, was called away on business, the two remaining batsmen had to pull out 28 runs, all thought of winning the match was given up; indeed, only nine more runs were made before the innings closed for the exceedingly small score of 23. As Friday was a batsman's day from the condition of the wicket, yesterday was all in favour of the bowlers, as will be seen by the accompanying analysis, the fine averages of both sides being remarkable, while the number of maiden overs shows most of the balls to have been well on the wicket.

——

No. 13 Match.

From the New York Herald, 14th & 15th September.

West Indians v. Staten Island.—Played at Staten Island on 13th and 14th September.

West Indians.

First Innings.		*Second Innings.*	
E. M. Skeete, b Pool	16	E. M. Skeete, b Pool	11
R. H. Stewart, b Lambkin	4	R. H. Stewart, b Pool	3
E. N. Marshall, b Butler	34	E. N. Marshall, b Massey	0
J. Lees, b Butler	9	J. Lees, b Pool	27
G. Wyatt, b Wilson	1	G. Wyatt, l b w, b Butle	16
W. H. Farquharson, b Butler	1	W. H. Farquharson, b Pool	19
L. Fyfe, not out	5	L. Fyfe, c Armstrong, b Butler	8
L. Kerr, b Wilson	1	L. Kerr, c Wilson, b Pool	11
P. A. Isaacs, run out	0	P. A. Isaacs, c Butler, b Pool	11
J. M. Burke, st. Lambkin, b Wilson	2	J. M. Burke, not out	11
T. Skeete, c Lambkin, b Wilson	0	T. Skeete, b Wilson	0
L. Isaacs, run out	0	L. Isaacs, run out	0
Extras	1	Extras	15
Total	74	Total	132

Staten Island.

First Innings.		*Second Innings.*	
J. R. Moore, c Kerr, b Burke	0	J. R. Moore, b Stewart	5
C. Wilson, st Kerr, b Stewart	20	Butler, not out	19
H. Clark, b Stewart	0	W. M. Massey, not out	9
Butler, c Fyfe, b Farquharson	21	C. Kessler, c Kerr, b Burke	5
W. M. Massey, b Stewart	48	G. E. Armstrong, b Burke	1
E. Kessler, b Farquharson	3	Extras	3
J. H. Lambkin, b T. Skeete	41		
J. L. Pool, c L. Isaacs, b Stewart	5		
R. R. MacGregor, b Farquharson	2		
A. C. Townsend, c Kerr, b Stewart	0		
G. E. Armstrong, not out	5		
W. K. Jewett, b Stewart	6		
Extras	14		
Total	165	Total	42

BOWLING ANALYSIS.

WEST INDIANS.

First Innings.	Balls	Mdns.	Rns.	Wkts.	*Second Innings.*	Balls	Mdns.	Rns.	Wkts.
Lambkin	48	7	21	1	Pool	132	23	35	6
Pool	60	7	22	1	MacGregor	40	4	15	0
MacGregor	36	4	9	0	Wilson	93	6	32	1
Butler	60	7	14	3	Butler	52	7	14	2
Wilson	39	4	7	4	Massey	64	11	5	1
					Kessier	24	2	16	0

STATEN ISLAND.

First Innings.	Balls	Mdns.	Rns.	Wkts.	*Second Innings.*	Balls	Mdns.	Rns.	Wkts.
Burke	84	8	44	1	Burke	44	3	18	2
Stewart	100	5	53	6	Stewart	40	2	19	1
Farquharson	80	8	32	3	Farquharson	2	0	2	0
Lees	28	1	20	0					
T. Skeete	16	2	2	1					

RUNS AT THE FALL OF EACH WICKET.

First Innings.

West Indians	7	37	55	63	66	67	68	68	74	74	74
Staten Island	6	17	38	54	57	135	141	150	152	152	165

Second Innings.

West Indians	35	41	42	50	64	87	94	96	118	129	132
Staten Island	6	11	12								

The majority of the West Indian cricketers who have been playing in the United States and Canada during the past month arrived here from Boston early yesterday morning, and at once proceeded to Staten Island. Their match yesterday was the last of their tour, and it was against the Staten Island Cricket Club, each side presenting twelve men. For the eleventh time in their schedule of thirteen matches did the lucky visitors win the toss, and Captain Laurence Fyfe, of Jamaica, said he would send his men to defend the wickets. The crease was wet and spongy at the start from the heavy rain of Sunday night; but under a bright sun and strong westerly wind it quickly dried and improved as the day wore on.

Beginning in Good Style.

The game was started at twenty minutes past twelve o'clock. E. M. Skeete and R. H. Stewart were first to assume the defensive, while J. H. Lambkin and J. L. Pool constituted the opening attack. Butler was at the wicket and G. E. Armstrong point. The first ball of Lambkin's fourth over clean bowled Stewart, who made way for E. N. Marshall, the score being 4. The associated batsmen between them lifted the score to 37, when Skeete, who had been playing easily and well, lost his wicket to Pool. J. Lees, who is considered the crack batsman of the West Indian team, and who has secured an average of over 30 runs on the tour, came next. Marshall showed careful and stubborn defence, which rang several changes in the bowling, MacGregor supplanting Lambkin, and Butler taking the ball from Pool, while Lambkin went behind the wickets. The score ran up to 55, when Lees lost his middle stump to the island professional. G. Wyatt, who was the originator of the West Indians' visit, came next. At this point Captain Cyril Wilson relieved MacGregor of the ball, and commenced bowling underhands. The change was astonishingly effective, for it was evident that the West Indians were unaccustomed to anything of the kind, either at home or since they have been abroad. Wyatt succumbed to an easy one, and W. H. Farquharson, the tall man of the team, took his place, only to be bowled by a slow round hand ball from Butler. Captain Fyfe was Marshall's fifth partner. When the latter had been two hours at the wickets, he also fell a victim to Butler. He had made 34, which included three 4 hits, a 3 and five 2's. L. L. Kerr was bowled by Wilson, Percy Isaacs and Captain Fyfe had a misunderstanding about a run, and the former was found out of his ground, while Burke was stumped by Lambkin off Wilson, and T. Skeete was caught by Lambkin off the same bowler. L. Isaacs was the last man, and he, like his cousin, was run out, leaving Captain Fyfe not out 5. The innings closed for 74, the seven last wickets only adding 11 runs between them to the score. The fielding of the home club was simply wretched, and it was an event when the ball did not go through their legs.

Staten Island's Turn.

The Staten Islanders then commenced their lucky innings. J. R. Moore and C. Wilson were the batsmen, Burke and Stewart bowling. The former was given out caught at the wicket, and Wilson was badly missed when he had made 6. Clarke came next and he followed Moore's lead in failing to score,

Stewart taking his wicket. With the total at 17, Butler came, and he and Wilson increased the score to 38, when the latter was neatly stumped by Kerr. He had made 20 by good hard hitting. Massey then came, and after Butler had hit an over-pitched ball from Farquharson, who was bowling in place of Burke, over the Club house, the latter was well caught by Captain Fyfe. Kessler, who was next, was out leg before wicket. The appearance of Lambkin was the signal for a big change in the big score. Between him and Massey 78 runs were put on. Massey batted most vigorously, and while he was missed badly when he made only 4, and twice, later on, by P. Isaacs, at deep square leg, he showed the best cricket of the day. His score of 48 contained eight 4 hits. Lambkin got 41, not altogether by safe play, and the rest of the side, which included J. L. Pool, R. R. MacGregor, A. C. Townsend and W. K. Jewett, were out for 13 runs. G. E. Armstrong was not out 5, and the innings closed for 165, or a lead of 91 on an even innings. The fast bowling of the visitors had been straight and fairly well maintained, while the brilliant fielding of Lees at cover point was well worth going far to see.

The match will be resumed this morning at eleven o'clock.

———

The two-days' match between the West Indians and the Staten Island Club was resumed yesterday at Livingston, S. I., and at the end of the day's play ended in a victory for the home team by nine wickets. This disastrous result was entirely due to the catches missed by the visiting team during the match. In other respects their fielding was excellent, their running and picking up being clean and their return quite good. At the commencement of operations yesterday, at 12 o'clock, the Staten Islanders had a lead of 91 runs on an even innings, the West Indians having scored 74 to their opponents' 165.

A Careful and Steady Beginning.

It was evident from the careful and steady way which the visitors opened their second innings that the endeavor to make the match a draw was not distant from their thoughts. E. Skeete and J. Lees were first at the wickets, while the bowling was in the hands of Pool and Wilson. The former sent down several maidens, but Wilson was hit about until 11 runs had been scored when Butler took his place. Runs came very slowly, and the first hour's play was only productive of a dozen notches. Five minutes later Kessler took the ball from Pool, but the change was not effective, as Lees drove him to the on for 3, and Skeete cracked him all about for singles. Again, and with the score at 20, another change was instituted in the trundling. MacGregor sending down the ball in place of Butler. The score continued to increase, and when it was 33, Massey relieved Kessler, and Pool resumed MacGregor's end. Then Pool bowled Skeete, who had been an hour securing his 11 runs. Stewart then joined Lees, and when the latter had put 21 to his credit he gave a hard catch to Wilson at mid-on, which was not accepted. Then there was some lively running for singles. When the score was 41 Pool toppled over Stewart's wicket, and Marshall filled the vacancy, but failed to score. Captain Fyfe was next, and after being badly missed by Armstrong at point he and Lees ran the score up to 50, when Lees, who had been showing great steadiness and very pretty form, was dismissed by a bailer from Pool. The outgoing batsman had made 27 runs, composed of two 4's, one 3, two 2's, and singles. P. Isaacs now joined Fyfe and opened his score with a grand leg hit for 4 off Pool. Massey in the meanwhile did some good bowling, sending down six maidens in succession. At 59 Wilson came on to bowl again in place of Massey, and five runs later Butler caught Isaacs, who was batting very patiently. Wyatt and Fyfe were then associated, and the run-getting proceeded at a snail's pace. Between them, however, they increased the score to 87, when the jolly Jamaican was caught at point by Armstrong. Farquharson then faced Wilson's underhands, and he sent the ball a-spinning. When Wyatt had by good along the ground driving got 16 he was given out leg before wicket. Isaacs came and was at once sharply run out by Butler, who caught the youngster napping outside of his ground. The score was 96 when Kerr joined Farquharson. The latter was hitting very hard to the on side, and one of his terrific smites came near removing the gaiters of a lady tennis player in a distant court. The century was passed and 118 was posted when Wilson caught Kerr at "silly point," as the Philadelphians call forward point close in. Burke came and Farquharson was neatly bowled by Pool. The giant's score of 19 was obtained by hard and correct hitting. Burke saw his other partner out with nothing to his name, and the innings closed at twenty minutes past four o'clock for 132 runs.

STATEN ISLAND TRIES AGAIN.

With forty-two runs to make to win and an hour and a half to play before time was called Staten Island started its second innings with Moore and

Armstrong defending the wickets. Then it was that the grit of the Indians was apparent. They made a very plucky fight and the best play altogether of the match was then witnessed. Burke and Stewart both bowled admirable and the ground fielding was very good, but the lack of "oil of palm" caused several catches to be missed that certainly should have been taken. Armstrong, being nearly bowled twice by Burke, was at last cooked. Moore was despatched by Stewart, and Kessler, who followed, was grandly caught at the wicket by Kerr. Three out for 12 runs. Then Butler and Murray were together. The former was missed three times, but Massey showed good form. Between the pair the necessary runs were secured, and the last match of the genial West Indians came to an end. Last evening they were entertained at a dinner given them by the Staten Islanders. To-day they sail for home, carrying with them the best wishes of all whom they met on the wickets in Yankeeland.

Visit of West Indian Gentlemen to Canada and the United States.

RESULT OF MATCHES.

MATCHES PLAYED 13; WON 6; DRAWN 2; LOST 5.

Opponents.	Where played.	When played.	West Indians.		Opponents.		Remarks.
			1st ins.	2nd ins.	1st ins.	2nd ins.	
Matches won (6)		1886.					*Won by*
Halifax Wanderers.........	Montreal	Aug. 18 & 19	319	...	113	64	an innings & 142 runs.
Ottawa C.C.	Ottawa	" 20 & 21	67	80	67	54	26 runs.
Toronto C.C.	Toronto	" 23 & 24	167	...	71	57	an innings & 39 runs.
Ontario Association XI ...	Toronto	" 25 & 26	51	109	101	43	16 runs.
Merion C.C. (return)......	Ardmore, Pa.	Sept. 1	*111	...	107	...	4 wickets, *6 w.d.
Longwood C.C.	Boston	" 10 & 11	97	39	95	23	18 runs.
Matches drawn (2)							*Remarks.*
Montreal C.C.	Montreal	Aug. 16 & 17	60	*101	112	130	*4 w.d.
Young America C.C.	Stenton, Pa.	Sept. 7 & 8	89	*175	284	...	*7 w.d.
Matches lost (5)							*Lost by*
Hamilton C.C.	Hamilton	Aug. 27 & 28	114	63	116	*63	7 wickets, *3 w.d.
Merion C.C.	Ardmore, Pa.	Aug. 31, & Sept. 1	54	36	86	*6	10 wickets, *no w.d.
Belmont C.C.	Elmwood, Pa.	Sept. 2 & 3	74	116	222	...	an innings & 32 runs.
Germantown C.C.	Nicetown, Pa.	" 4 & 6	74	148	310	...	an innings & 88 runs.
Staten Island C.C.	Staten Island, N.Y.	" 13 & 14	74	132	165	*42	8 wickets, *3 w.d.

A curious coincidence is the fact that in the 5 matches lost, the total of each of our first innings ended with the figure 4; three, of the five, each giving the same total of 74.

BATTING AVERAGES.

Names.	Matches batted in.	Innings commenced.	Times not out.	Times, How out. Bowled.	Caught.	L.B.W.	Hit wkt.	Run out.	Stump'd.	Largest innings.	Total runs scored.	Average runs per innings.
1. Jack Lees.......	13	23	2	9	11	1	–	–	–	47	466	22.4
2. E. N. Marshall ..	10	17	1	11	4	–	–	1	–	47	231	14.7
3. E. M. Skeete....	11	20	1	8	9	–	–	2	–	32	245	12.17
4. W. H. Farqu'son .	13	23	–	10	9	–	–	3	1	55	265	11.12
5. J. M. Burke	12	19	6	4	6	–	–	1	2	45	136	10.6
6. G. Wyatt......	10	18	1	7	6	3	–	–	1	64	166	9.13
7. Percy Isaacs....	8	13	1	4	4	2	–	2	–	21	88	7.4
8. R. H. Stewart ...	13	22	–	10	9	–	–	1	2	17	146	6.14
9. A. W. Swain	7	11	1	5	5	–	–	–	–	27	54	5.4
10. T. S. Skeete	7	13	3	4	5	–	–	1	–	*19	53	5.3
11. Leo Isaacs	10	17	2	9	4	–	–	2	–	*26	71	4.11
12. Louis Kerr.....	8	14	1	6	7	–	–	–	–	12	61	4.9
13. W. O. Collymore	6	10	2	4	4	–	–	–	–	12	35	4.3
14. L. R. Fyfe......	13	22	3	6	13	–	–	–	–	8	61	3.4

*Means not out.

Summary.—14 men played in 242 innings.—"Not Outs", numbered 24=218 complete innings for a total of 2,078 runs; average per man per innings 9.116.

97	were	bowled
96	"	caught
6	"	Leg before
13	"	Run out
6	"	Stumped
218		

BOWLING AVERAGES.

Names.	Matches bowled in.	No. of overs bowled.	Maiden overs.	Runs scored.	How taken.				Total wickets taken.	Average runs per wicket.
					Bowled.	Caught.	L.B.W.	Stump'd.		
W. H. Farquharson	13	386^{1}	152	565	34	25	1	1	61	9.16
R. H. Stewart	12	232	72	397	22	12	...	8	42	9.19
J. M. Burke	12	487^{2}	214	651	29	35	1	...	65	10.1
T. S. Skeete	3	10	3	12	1	...	...	...	1	12
Jack Lees	11	177^{3}	47	339	8	7	...	4	19	17.16
E. N. Marshall	5	49	19	73	1	1	1	...	3	24.1
Leo Isaacs	3	22	7	42	1	...	...	...	1	42
A. W. Swain	3	33	13	60	...	...	...	...	0	...

Wide Balls:—Skeete, 1; Farquharson, 1; Burke, 2. = 4.

No Balls:—None.

Summary:—8 men bowled 1397 overs (of which 527 were maidens) and took 192 wickets for a total of 2,139 runs. Average runs per wicket 11.27.

SUNDRY SCRAPS OF INFORMATION.

Wicket-keeping.

		Stumped.	Caught.
L. L. Kerr, 5 matches	...	... 5	13 = 18
P. Isaacs 5 "	...	... 5	6 = 11
G. Wyatt 3 "	...	... 3	2 = 5

Professionals against us.

Lacey for Montreal	Bradley for Belmont
Morley for Merion	Chambers for Longwood
Butler for Staten Island.	

Highest wins.
West Indians....—An innings and 142 runs, v. Halifax Wanderers.
Opponents......—An innings and 88 runs, Germantown.

Highest scores in one innings.
West Indians....—319, v Halifax Wanderers.
Opponents......—310, Germantown C.C.

Smallest scores in one innings.
West Indians....—36, v. Merion C.C.
Opponents......—23, Longwood C.C.

Highest individual scores in an innings.
West Indians....—Mr. G. Wyatt 64, v. Young America.
Opponents......—Mr. W. C. Morgan 85, for Germantown.

Extras.
West Indians gave away 196.
Opponents   "   " 181.

Total runs (including extras).

West Indians....—2,350 for 224 wickets, average 10.110.
Opponents......—2,331 for 203 wickets, average 11.98.

Gate money received.

In Canada:—

Montreal	4 days	...	...$ 20 75	
Ottawa	2 " ...	...	... none	
Toronto	4 " ...	...	... 26 75	
Hamilton	2 " ...	...	... 31 00	$78 50

In the United States:—

Merion	2 days ...		...$ 39 00	
Belmont	2 " ...	...	... 50 00	
Germantown	2 " ...	...	... 59 00	
Young America	2 " ...	...	... 22 50	
Longwood	2 " ...	...	... none	
Staten Island	2 " ...	...	... none	$170 50
Total	...	...	...	$249 00

Personnel of the Team.

———

Jack Lees (Jamaica) was without doubt by far and away the best all-round cricketer. As a batsman, no one came anywhere near him, and he deserved many more runs for his steady, consistent play. In the field he was excellent at all points, and if the "catching" capabilities of the team had been up to the mark he would have been more successful at bowling.

E. N. Marshall (Jamaica), though not a stylish batsman, was very lucky and turned out a most useful man. A very fair field, but not much of a bowler.

E. M. Skeete (Barbados) established his reputation as a very useful bat; is a very active and energetic field, and was especially good at longstop whenever one was used. If he sticks to the game regularly he will turn out a first-rate cricketer.

W. H. Farquharson (Jamaica) stands first in bowling averages, though, had Burke a little less, and Stewart a little more, work, the places of the three would have been changed. They all certainly did well in bowling. A very good bat, though cramped at times. His height, 6 ft. 4 in., gives him a splendid reach and he can hit very hard. Unfortunately he is a very poor field.

J. M. Burke (Jamaica), the youngest of the team, did well, and promises good things in the future both in bowling and batting. He should certainly cultivate more activity in the field.

G. Wyatt (Demerara) made highest individual score. A fair bat, but six "ducks" (four consecutively) spoilt his average: for his local club he headed the list this season with 2015. Kept wickets a little, and was fairly good in the field.

Percy Isaacs (Jamaica) has a very good style but came off very badly in batting: did well at wicket-keeping, but at catches in the out-field was at times unaccountably unlucky.

R. H. Stewart (Demerara) was most successful with his slow over-arm bowling with good break from leg. A very active, sharp, and, as a rule, clean field. Is a good bat, but was sadly out of form.

A. W. Swain (Demerara) was unlucky in his three attempts at bowling, as catches were missed off him each time : in the Germantown match, when the largest score against us was made and the batsmen well set, he bowled 25 overs, 10 of which were maidens. For his local club his average for this season reads, 157 overs, 40 maidens, 363 runs, 42 wickets: average 8.27. An active field; throws well and with precision. Wants more practice at batting.

T. S. SKEETE (Barbados): A steady but not elegant bat, was in want of practice; his score in the match at Boston was very useful. Bowled on three occasions only; might have been made more use of.

Leo ISAACS (Jamaica): Left-handed. Seemed unlucky at batting. Fair field; and bowled on three occasions, without, however, much success.

LOUIS KERR (Demerara) was unfortunately very ill at Barbados on the way from Demerara to New York, and was far from well at any time during the tour. Though really an excellent bat, he did nothing. As wicket-keeper, however, he was far the best of the three, and showed to perfection in the last two matches of the tour, stumping 5 and catching 7.

W. O. COLLYMORE (Barbados) played the fewest number of times of any of the men. He was unsuccessful at scoring. A very fair field, and held some good catches.

L. R. FYFE (Jamaica), our "evergreen skipper," seemed most unlucky (except as regards tossing for innings) during the whole tour, never having been successful in getting into double figures: in one match he batted over an hour for three runs. In the field he held some fine catches at point and cover.

———

"A FEW NOTES."

———

By another of them.

———

The account of our tour has already extended to considerable length, principally on account of the newspaper reports of our matches being included, which many friends wished for and all of us decided to have; some with a special view of having a permanent record of many of the curious phrases contained therein and others for the favourable and unfavourable opinions expressed about us as cricketers, &c. Were we able to give the large type headings of the newspaper accounts of the matches, they would amuse some of our readers very much, but doubtless the numerous newspaper cuttings collected by most of us have already been perused by many intimate friends with keen enjoyment.

It remains for me therefore to be brief.

The attempt of a West Indian team visiting Canada and the United States was sneered and laughed at by many more than most people imagine, as rather a farce;—it has been done, though not as successfully as the players themselves could have wished, but looking at the team that actually represented the West Indians as compared with one that might have done so the result on this basis may be considered fairly satisfactory.

Apart from poor representation the expense of the tour amounted to something very near £1000 in all, which (less small amounts subscribed in Jamaica and Barbados, hardly it is presumed £150 together) has been virtually paid by the men themselves. An average, however, of £71 or $340 per man in round figures for 8 or 9 weeks holiday, though six days cricket per week while ashore is no light work, is not out of the way. Of course, the cost for Demerara and Barbados men amounted to more than those from Jamaica, on account of the shorter journey of the latter. Gate-money was received, though the writer was very much against it from the first, but it only amounted to about £50 between fourteen of us. Let us hope that on future occasions it will not be taken by visiting teams. Certainly, if we had come off as well as the Englishmen in 1885, it would have been a welcome help especially to some of us, but this season (1886) the Englishmen fared much worse than in 1885, the falling off being something like fifty per cent.

The ball has been set a-rolling now, and if the result of our recent tour gives us many visits in the West Indies from our Canadian and American friends, and wakes up our Island neighbours and our own Colony to move about amongst each other and further a-field, in the interest of the "noble game," something tangible and well worth having will have been gained, and the writer fully and well recompensed for what trouble he has taken in the matter.

But a hint to our Island neighbours must be given. Some proper and really strong move must be made to secure permanent and good cricket grounds everywhere in the West Indies where the game is to take any standing, and let us hope that nowhere will this latter not be the case. In Barbados especially, the rendezvous and head quarters for all passenger steamers, there ought certainly to be the best ground in the West Indies, and we trust that the "blot" (for such it is) of not having such a ground will not continue much longer.

G. W.

Demerara, 20th December, 1886.